The
Right Choice

The
Right Choice

*A Complete Guide to Evaluating,
Selecting, and Installing
MRP II Software*

Christopher D. Gray

THE *Oliver Wight* ® COMPANIES

*Oliver Wight Limited Publications, Inc.
5 Oliver Wight Drive
Essex Junction, VT 05452*

Library of Congress Catalog Card Number: 86-63916

Copyright © 1987 by Oliver Wight Limited Publications, Inc.

ISBN: 0-939246-09-0

Manufactured in the United States of America by
The Maple-Vail Book Manufacturing Group.

1 2 3 4 5 6 7 8 9 10

This book is dedicated to the memory of
James F. McLaughlin
my friend, a true manufacturing professional, and
an MRP II pioneer

Contents

Acknowledgments

Many people contributed to the writing of *The Right Choice,* and deserve my thanks. Within the Oliver Wight Companies, I'd like to express my appreciation to John Civerolo, Bob Stahl, and Tom Wallace, who worked with me on a "software starter kit" project for client companies in 1984 and 1985. Much of the material and the ideas that were discussed as part of that project eventually evolved into material for this book. John Dougherty and Norris Edson are two top professionals with whom I've been associated since the mid 70s, and who have influenced my thinking on software significantly. Dave Garwood constantly challenges my understanding of the role of software and software vendors in the successful implementation of MRP II. John DeVito teaches the Oliver Wight Systems and Data Processing classes with me, and was involved in the development of much of the classroom material that was incorporated in the following pages. Pete Skurla reviewed the first "complete" manuscript and made a number of valuable comments that were incorporated into the final document.

Thanks also to Dana Scannell, my publisher, and Bill Farragher, our public relations counsel, both of whom encouraged me to write the book—Bill for more years than he probably wishes to remember. And thanks to Jennifer Smith and Valerie Rochon, who were involved in the initial discussion of content, and who made a number of helpful suggestions on the organization and approach of *The Right Choice*.

All of these people made contributions to the manuscript, but three individuals deserve special mention. Oliver Wight, though not a "data processing professional" as the term is commonly used, understood more about management systems and data processing effectiveness than anyone else I've ever known. The germs of many of my ideas and my understanding of systems can be traced back to Ollie's writings and teachings. Darryl Landvater, my friend and partner in Oliver Wight Software Research for many years, has been a patient teacher and helpful critic. Without his advice and assistance over the years, this book would never have been written. Finally, Steve Bennett, a professional writer, forced me to sharpen my ideas, helped me shape them into readable English sentences, and forced me to stick to my timetable for producing the manuscript.

And last, but certainly not the least, a deeply grateful thank you to my wife, Allison—who, as a purchasing professional and MRP II user, provided helpful comments on the material and truly enhanced the quality of the book—and my two sons, Patrick and Colin. As any author knows, surviving a book requires a patient family that can understand and support the loss of time that would otherwise be spent with two young sons.

The
Right Choice

Introduction

He who hesitates is lost.
(An old truism)

In today's manufacturing world, just about everyone knows that an effective MRP II system means increased efficiency, less waste, and greater profits. Unfortunately, many people assume that to achieve those benefits, all they have to do is buy the right software package, install it on their computer, and then sit back as the balance sheet soaks up black ink. It's not that easy. MRP II is an essential management tool, not a magic pill for eliminating the challenges and hard work necessary for running a manufacturing operation. Moreover, managing effectively using the tools of an MRP II system does not happen on its own, just as excellent quality, management stability, strong positive leadership, and consistent organizational values do not materialize out of thin air. All result from the concerted efforts of dedicated people.

Similarly, operating MRP II goes far beyond running software on a computer. It really means changing the behavior of people in the organization, getting senior managers to agree to a set of high-level plans that can be broken down into specific tasks and objectives, and then holding people accountable for executing them. As a result, the software, although an important prerequisite for doing MRP II, turns out to be the least critical part of an operating system.

So why a whole book on MRP II software? There are three impor-

3

tant reasons. First, though software is but one part of an effective MRP II system, it is a critical component; problem software can sabotage the rest of your MRP efforts. The right software, on the other hand, can eliminate many of the common technical obstacles to reaching Class A levels of performance.

Second, no other aspect of implementing MRP II is more likely to generate high emotion levels than software evaluation and selection. For some reason, otherwise rational individuals often draw their swords to defend their favorite software package, and as they fight a duel to the death the least important element of the system winds up causing the greatest number of problems and delays.

Finally, for most companies the software purchase and software selection process represents the most expensive part of implementing MRP. Mainframe MRP II software costs upwards of one million dollars, and most companies looking at this software spend 12 to 18 months evaluating different alternatives. Minicomputer software, though less expensive ($75,000 to $500,000), often requires nine to 12 months of evaluation time. Microcomputer MRP II software, ranging from $10,000 to $50,000 per package, typically consumes six to nine months before a decision is made.

Despite the expense, many companies evaluate and select their software without truly understanding what it takes to make MRP II work effectively, and without making the proper commitment to getting the system on the air. As a result, as several studies have shown, the cost of making the software purchasing decision often exceeds the cost of the actual software *by a factor of about five*.

To understand why this happens, think about the history of the computer in business. Since the early days of computers, manufacturing companies have been automating their accounting functions. Payroll was a popular application for companies installing their first computer. "We'll eliminate two or three payroll clerks, and realize significant savings," they said. Yet although the new system worked just fine, few could point to more than meager savings; when they eliminated the three payroll clerks, they added a computer programmer, a computer operator, and a keypuncher operator, none of whom were volunteers.

Such unrealized paybacks have made many senior managers skeptical of any new systems that purport to yield high payback. Consequently, they feel no pressure to bring truly valuable systems on the air, and the process of selecting a package can drag on far longer than it should.

But the financial realities of MRP are truly different from most other systems. Twenty years of implementing and operating MRP and MRP II systems demonstrate that the payback from effective planning and scheduling is not only quantifiable, but astronomical! A survey conducted in 1985 by the Oliver Wight Companies indicates that an average MRP/MRP II user reduces inventory 17 percent, improves customer service 16 percent, increases productivity 10 percent, and reduces purchase costs 7 percent.

For Class A performers, the numbers are even more impressive: inventory reduction 25 percent, customer service improvement 28 percent, productivity increases 16 percent, and purchase cost reductions 11 percent. These statistics translate into an outstanding 200 percent return on investment. For a sixty million dollar company, the benefit from MRP/MRP II is a staggering *$100,000 per month!*

Interestingly, the significant software costs for most companies have nothing to do with the purchase price—the real cost stems from delaying the project by six, nine, or 12 months. If the software selection process were cut to three to four months, without compromising the effectiveness of the decision, the resulting savings to a $60,000,000 company would be as high as *$900,000.*

The good news is that the evaluation and selection process for MRP II software need not take more than a few months. *The Right Choice* offers you a time-tested approach to making an intelligent purchasing decision within that time-frame, and is based on the experience of hundreds of companies[1] that have successfully used MRP II during the past decade. Before we begin discussing the software selection process, take a moment to review what this book is designed to do.

The Right Choice assumes that the reader is familiar with the mechanics and the principles of MRP II. Readers who require additional

---

[1] The case studies and examples in the following pages are based on incidents at actual companies. The names of the companies, and in some instances the exact circumstances of the incident, have been changed so that the companies cannot be easily identified.

details should study Appendix A, which provides an overview of the functions of an MRP II system. Appendix B is a selected bibliography of MRP literature, while Appendix C lists sources of additional information.

The Right Choice is intended to be a comprehensive discussion of the issues you need to consider in determining which software programs will best meet your company's needs, in avoiding common pitfalls that can lead to costly delays, and in determining which functions in the software are missing, need to be modified, or should be eliminated. It is not a book on the architecture or programming details of an MRP II system. Since program design and architectural issues are important in determining the proper software for a company, the reader is urged to refer to a widely accepted standard for MRP II software, a research document entitled the *MRP II Standard System*, which is published by Oliver Wight Software Research, Inc. and is offered as part of its services.

It should also be pointed out that *The Right Choice* does not cover implementation issues beyond those related to hardware or software. The now-famous MRP II Implementation Plan, authored by Darryl Landvater, is provided in Appendix D, and a reader needing additional information should read an excellent book entitled *MRP II: Making It Happen* by Thomas F. Wallace (see Appendix B).

The philosophy of *The Right Choice* is that there are no instant answers to the problem of finding the best MRP software package for your company. Note that the term "best" is used only in the context of "your company." There is no "best" MRP package in an objective sense—each one has its strong and weak points, and the main objective is to find one that will work for you and then get it on the air without surprises or delays. That means conducting careful research on the packages that appear to be reasonably complete, compatible with the existing technical environment and simple enough to be fixed or interfaced with existing systems.

Finally, although I cannot guarantee that by reading *The Right Choice* you will reach Class A levels of performance, the fact is that a number of companies have used the principles described in the following pages to achieve Class A results. Many have done so in record time.

The ultimate goal of this book is to provide you with the guidelines and conceptual tools you need for getting through the software selection process with as little hesitation as possible. And when it comes to MRP II, the less you hesitate, the less you lose.

Christopher D. Gray
November 1986
Newfields, NH

Chapter 1

Of Dreams and Reality:

The Hard Facts About MRP Software

If anything can go wrong, it will.
(Murphy's Law)

Just two decades ago, if you wanted to do MRP, you either wrote your own program, or you bought IBM's Production Information and Control System ("PICS"). The choice was that simple, the options that limited. The situation has changed quite a bit since then; the number of commercially available MRP and MRP II packages has grown by nearly 20 percent per year, with nearly 200 to choose from today. In fact, the problem facing most companies today is not the lack of choices, but rather the overwhelming number of choices, especially if they have no hardware to constrain them. Unless a company owns an ENIAC 4000B, there is probably an off-the-shelf MRP II package or two that will run on it.

While commercial MRP II software packages do differ in technology, human engineering, simplicity, price, and sometimes integration with other vendor-supplied systems, most of the more popular packages are similar in terms of the essential functions needed for MRP II. For example, while the popular MRP II packages for the IBM mainframe look different on the surface, they are virtual clones of each other when it comes to basic functionality.

This likeness among MRP II packages is to be expected, because the market for MRP II systems has matured, and MRP II has become the normal way of running a manufacturing or distribution business. In fact, given the widespread acceptance of the principles of MRP II, one would be more surprised if the various software vendors did *not* provide a common set of functions. Competition has also helped in this regard, as it has forced vendors to conform to recognized minimum standards for MRP II functionality.

The fact is, no MRP II software package will break much new ground today—the collective experience of companies during the 1960s and 1970s has identified a basic logic and set of functions needed to run MRP, and any successful MRP II program will merely be an expression of that core thinking. This is not to say that there is no room for innovation. It does mean, though, that real innovation has to be separated from what may amount to someone's first crack at solving an old functional problem. Real innovation is more likely to be in areas such as human engineering, so that people have faster and easier access to the information within their systems, and integration with customer and vendor systems (e.g. an integrated supply chain from manufacturing to retail distribution).

The fact that MRP II software is functionally similar and is based on a standard logic brings us to another key point: the MRP II systems used by various Class A companies are likewise similar, even when the brand of hardware and the core of packaged software functions used are different. This point is brought home by an incident in 1975 in which consultant George Bevis, then a senior vice president of The Tennant Company, hosted a visit from a company that wanted to see how Tennant carried out its world-renowned MRP II operation. Bevis's visitors became noticeably perplexed when the tour ended and they had not been shown the computer room. "But what *kind* of system do you use?" they asked uneasily. Bevis scratched his chin and then threw up his hands, saying, "It's blue."

The moral is that the computer could have just as well been red, black, green, or paisley because it and its associated software are just tools. Just as woodworking tools are essential to cabinet making, software is essential to operating MRP II. In each case, the tools in and of themselves are not sufficient to generate results; neither woodworking tools nor MRP II software can impart skill to the unskilled. The effectiveness ultimately depends on the knowledge and abilities of the user.

But if MRP software is nothing more than a standardized tool, isn't the selection of MRP II software an arbitrary process? And isn't it a waste of time to carefully evaluate and select MRP software when the implementation results are likely to be the same?

The answer to both questions is "no." Even though, as we shall soon see, all MRP II packages have problems, some are more easily modified than others to give you the minimum set of desired functionality, and some are more easily interfaced to existing systems. It is, therefore, worth spending some time determining which packages will cause you the fewest delays in bringing MRP on air. It is also worth taking the time to plan for the systems and data processing effort that will be required to modify the new package or interface it to existing systems. Again, experience shows that being able to anticipate the problems and efforts associated with an MRP package rather than reacting to them is the key to a swift implementation.

Before looking at specific points related to the evaluation and selection of MRP II software, it's essential to develop a realistic perspective on the overall evaluation process. Consider the following misconceptions:

Dream #1:
We'll take it home and plug it in.

Reality #1:
Yes, we have no "plain vanilla" installations today.

I've been researching software for nearly a decade, and have often found that people's attitude toward packaged MRP II software is similar to their attitude toward appliances. That is, purchasing MRP II software is like buying a washing machine: you take delivery, open the box, plug it in, and then begin using it.

I'm sorry to say that it's not that simple. Even the most complete MRP II package has some functional deficiencies or needs to be modified to meet the regulatory requirements of certain industries. And

most companies have a few specialized needs that must be met. Therefore, the chances of finding a package that satisfies all the functions of
MRP II plus each and every specialized requirement is probably small.
Even if such a package were to be found, as you'll read below, there
would be some serious implications to a software design philosophy
that tries to satisfy every conceivable requirement. There will be bugs,
too, especially when the package is new. The package may also be
difficult to interface with your company's existing systems, or it may
be difficult to interface temporarily during the transition period.

In some respects, though, software and software suppliers are merely
products of the marketplace, and the buyers are in part to blame for
software problems. No software vendor today is held to the high standards that are expected from appliance, electronics, or industrial
equipment manufacturers. In fact, software users have actually come
to accept that they may be purchasing incomplete and possibly even
faulty products. The absurdity of the situation is underscored by the
warranties on most microcomputer packages, which guarantee the
physical condition of the diskette, but offer no promises as to whether
the software does what it is supposed to do, or that it won't damage
your data—in effect, no warranty at all.

Caveat emptor certainly applies to minicomputer and mainframe
packages as well. Take the case of a major hardware vendor which, in
the mid-1970s, began feeling pressure to upgrade its MRP package so
that it could compete more effectively with other vendors who offered
"new and innovative" features. The company set out to develop the
ultimate MRP II package in terms of state-of-the-art technology and
functionality and, because of its track record in the data processing
services field, was able to sign up nearly 30 customers even though the
package was still little more than an idea. When the software was
actually released, it was, as the company promised, jam-packed with
features. But it was also loaded with bugs and functional problems.
The fact that net change MRP took 35 hours to run on one client's pilot
product line was the least of the problems; the fact that it frequently
aborted in the middle of certain jobs was real cause for concern.

Eventually, many of the problems of this "ultimate" MRP package
were fixed, but the overall costs to the customers were enormous, and
the damage to the vendor's reputation and future MRP software sales

may be permanent. While the vendor is certainly culpable for rushing a product to market without adequate quality control, *the people who purchased this package were equally irresponsible* because they bought on the basis of promises—without testimony from successful users, independent analysis, or published reviews.

The corollary to *caveat emptor*, then, is to be a *responsible consumer*. That means learning everything you can about how well a particular product has been tested, under what conditions, who uses it already and what their experience with the system has been, whether there are known and outstanding bugs, and whether it meets objective criteria for an MRP II system.

In many cases, and for most software vendors, there *will* have been adequate amounts of testing, and there *will* be successful users, and there *won't* be overwhelming numbers of problems, and the software *will* be reasonably functional. In my experience, the majority of software vendors are responsible, professional, customer oriented—and can be a major help in eliminating software as a problem in implementing MRP II. For example, there are a number of instances I know of where software companies have gone "beyond the call of duty" to assist client companies in solving implementation and installation problems.

And I've had many good experiences with vendors who responded quickly to correct deficiencies in their software once those deficiencies were known. For example, in the late 1970s, I did an evaluation of a popular minicomputer-based MRP II system. At the time, the software was missing some basic functionality for MRP II, including firm planned orders and master production scheduling, so that a large part of the time I spent with the vendor was spent discussing these functions. Yet instead of trying to hide the missing functionality, or being defensive about the system, or even trying to rationalize the missing capabilities (any of which could easily have happened), the vendor took the discussion in a very positive way, and committed to fixing the deficiencies. Within a year, the company had made three major releases that included a complete master production scheduling system, firm planned orders, and a number of helpful improvements to the system!

Sadly, in a small number of instances, there will be problems with the vendor or with the software that could have been avoided if sufficient checking had been done in the beginning. Many of the illustrations and examples in this book cover these types of situations—not because these situations are common or normal (they are not), but rather because in the small number of cases where there is a problem vendor or problem software, an astute purchaser can usually find out in advance just by knowing what types of problems do occur and what questions to ask. Think about it this way: in every type of business there are good vendors and there are bad vendors—in fact, it's probably a bell-shaped curve, with the worst vendors to the left of the norm, and the very best vendors to the right of the norm. Every customer owes it to himself to try to do business with a vendor that is better, not worse, than average. In order to find vendors that are to the right of the norm, a buyer needs to know the kinds of problems that can be recognized and anticipated before making a major commitment. So the intent of the examples in this book is to identify the types of problems that can be anticipated and arm you with the knowledge of how to avoid them—not to damn the software companies in general because of the actions of only a few.

An example of a series of problems that could be avoided occurred recently when one of our client companies asked us to evaluate a new MRP package that looked promising but did not have a long history or proven track record. My friend and professional associate Bob Stahl and I did a documentation review just prior to flying out for a meeting with the software vendor. Based on the documentation, the logic and functionality of the system appeared sound, although there were a number of open issues because of the lack of sample reports, report formats, and test output. In a meeting to discuss the logic of the system, we requested such sample reports and test output as a way to verify the logic of the software. After hours of hedging, the software vendor finally produced a set of the requested reports, including samples of the MRP report, master production schedule, dispatch list, capacity requirements planning report, and order status displays. Just as we were beginning to suspect from the vendor's actions, the reports indicated a system loaded with serious errors, which the vendor initially explained as "corrupt test data." After being further pressed, however, the vendor admitted that the product had not been tested, that it had been released without effective quality controls (nearly 20 companies had received copies of the system), and as a result had numerous bugs. In fact, in the two years since the meeting, the vendor has failed to convince us that the problems have been resolved in the standard version of the software.

So why all the quality control problems with this vendor and the one cited earlier? In fairness to the software vendors, MRP II software packages are huge by software standards. A typical mainframe system often exceeds one million lines of COBOL statements. And even in the simplest system, testing all the combinations and permutations of features and functions is an enormously challenging task. In the more complex systems, the vendors can only test a small subset of the processing logic, and must assume that if it is in good working order, the rest of the system will be too. If your needs happen to fall within the subset of functions tested, you may have software that performs properly. If not, you may have trouble.

On the other hand, commercial airliners are also large systems, and we demand them to be defect free. No one would even consider stepping foot on a jumbo jet if he or she knew that the manufacturer had tested only the "normal" functions of the system, and that the passengers were expected to test the majority of the functions themselves under working conditions. An extreme comparison? Perhaps. But it is useful in demonstrating that size and complexity are not a barrier to adequate quality control and product testing.

The bottom line is that *a responsible consumer, no matter how well he may have evaluated and selected MRP software, should be prepared for problems and modifications that will have to be tackled by his systems and data processing staff*. One possible exception may be the very small company getting into MRP for the first time, where a small number of people and fairly complete software may add up to a relatively pain-free installation. The typical company, however, must anticipate a significant systems and data processing effort in one or more of the following areas:

1. Temporary interfaces to systems that will eventually be replaced.
2. Permanent interfaces to systems that are not being replaced.
3. Modifications to the software package.
4. Fixes to bugs.

Figure 1.1 illustrates the amount of relative effort that different types of companies will probably expend in systems and data processing.

COMPANY SIZE	TYPICAL SITUATION	TYPES OF SYSTEMS AND DP EFFORT REQUIRED (RANKED)
Very small (less than $10M)	Manual systems, little computerization	1. Few changes or interface if a fairly complete system can be found. May use report writer for custom reporting
Small ($10M to $50M)	Some systems in place. Often financials and MRP subsystems, purchasing	1. Modifications 2. Temporary interfaces 3. Permanent interfaces 4. Bug fixes
Medium ($50M to $250M)	Generally financial systems, MRP subsystems, purchasing, some downstream applications	1. Temporary interfaces 2. Modifications 3. Permanent interfaces 4. Bug fixes
Large (more than $250M)	Many financial and accounting systems, many manufacturing applications including subsystems, some of the downstream applications, some planning and scheduling logic	1. Temporary interfaces 2. Permanent interfaces 3. Modifications 4. Bug fixes

Figure 1.1
Relative effort expended in systems and data processing

Dream #2:
All we need is the right software to succeed.

Reality #2:
People make systems work.

Since the earliest days of computers and computer systems, the role of people has been misplaced. We've had twenty years of "factory of the future," "automated factory," and CIM (computer integrated manufacturing) articles in the business press, all hinting that at some point human beings would be virtually eliminated from manufacturing processes.

In reality, the factory of the future that's based on high tech gimmickery looks as far off today as it did two decades ago. In a revealing article in *Fortune* magazine (November 10, 1986), author Anne B. Fisher explains why General Motors' much publicized investment in robots, computers, lasers, etc. has not yielded the expected payback: "What went wrong became apparent when managers at GM took a close look at New United Motor Manufacturing Inc., Nummi for short, the GM-Toyota joint venture that turns out the Corolla-based Chevy Nova. Although Nummi's humble Fremont, California, factory hasn't been stuffed with fancy robotics or other high-tech marvels, its productivity is about twice that of most GM plants, and its Novas have earned the highest customer-satisfaction ratings and lowest warranty costs of any GM car. The reason: Japanese-style management and a labor agreement that made it possible (*Fortune*, July 9, 1986). Hoping to replicate Nummi's performance on a wider scale, GM has been dispatching hundreds of managers from Detroit and elsewhere around the country to Fremont for a good look around. Many have come back convinced that Nummi's way of managing workers can do more good for GM than all the world's lasers and robots. Nummi's lesson, as Ross Perot puts it, is that 'brains and wits will beat capital spending ten times out of ten.' "

In other words, experience demonstrates that simple tools used by properly motivated and educated people who can work together as a team—not fancy hardware or software, sophisticated algorithms, or mathematical hocus pocus—add up to high levels of management effectiveness. There is no software equivalent to a magic wand.

Accordingly, to get anything at all out of software for MRP II, be aware that education is a prerequisite to improvement. And in this case, "education" means more than just pumping people full of facts and terms—it entails behavior modification, teamwork, and accountability for results. Figure 1.2 lists some of the more common behaviors that must be changed for MRP to succeed.

If you can modify the way people do their work and relate to the system, remarkable feats can be achieved. In fact you can use the least

PRIOR BEHAVIOR	MODIFIED BEHAVIOR
Issue edicts: Cut inventory 10%	Use the sales and operating plan to manage inventory reductions
Sign all purchase orders over $1000	Create a valid master schedule, check the critical measurements
Personally expedite a best customer's order	Use the master schedule to set priorities in the factory
Overload the master schedule by 25–30% to "give them an incentive"	Create a do-able master schedule within resource constraints and hold people accountable for executing it
Estimate cash requirements by taking current plus past due purchase orders, multiplying by 60%	Use the actual numbers from the system to calculate precise cash requirements
Fudge the forecast because of past performance problems in manufacturing	Tell the truth about what you expect to sell—if that changes, update the forecast right away
Make up shortage lists to identify the "real priorities"	Work to the dispatch list
Make sure that today's crisis is fixed, worry about tomorrow tomorrow	Work just as hard to eliminate problems in the future as you do to fix today's crisis
Read dropping queues as "layoff coming," slow down so output drops	Understand that queues can be managed, that smaller not larger queues are generally better, and that the company may have to operate at lower queue levels

Figure 1.2
Common behavior prior to and after MRP II

functional software and get to Class A levels of performance. Look at how successful some companies have been with the old IBM PICS package. PICS is not only functionally incomplete, it is difficult to use and modify. Yet a number of companies have reached Class A levels of performance with PICS and today enjoy the full benefits of MRP. At the same time, many companies have implemented some of the more modern, more complete systems and have never gotten close to achieving their anticipated benefits.

While PICS would not be the program of choice in the 1980s, there are some valuable lessons that one can learn from the Class A companies that did implement it in the past:

1. Putting your time and energy into the user area pays off. The companies that implemented PICS wisely considered education to be a key component of successful MRP.
2. Knowing the limitations of your software makes for a speedier implementation. Companies that implemented PICS in 1972 knew that they were buying just a shell that lacked fundamental features. They had no preconceived notions about what the software could do and were able to focus their attention on essential additions and changes that needed to be made.
3. Learning from other people's experience can save you a great deal of money and effort. PICS users greatly benefitted from a now-famous conference in 1972 hosted by Oliver Wight and George Plossl and sponsored by APICS. During the conference, various sites exchanged ideas about their successes and failures with MRP, which meant that each one didn't have to reinvent the wheel. For example, one participant, Markem Corporation, had earlier identified the need for a projected on-hand balance display in the MRP reports in PICS, and had written a subroutine that could be called from the report program. Their program was made part of the 1972 conference proceedings so that others could use it, too. Today, any company can share its experiences and learn from others through various classes and seminars, and can likewise benefit from a greater pool of knowledge.
4. Having fewer options is a blessing (see Dream/Reality #4). Since the PICS package was a "bare bones" approach that required customers to fill in the missing functions, users wound up focusing their energy on creating only those subsystems that they actually needed. Moreover, because of their education effort, these companies had people who served as "checks and balances" to ensure that no one was writing unnecessary modules. Again, it is the people factor that makes the difference.

Dream #3:

The more time we spend evaluating software, the less time we'll have to spend implementing MRP II.

Reality #3:

After some point, implementation time is directly proportional to software evaluation time.

Ironically, companies that spend the most time evaluating software seem to be the last ones to get the desired results. A protracted search for the perfect MRP software package tends to:

1. Divert people from the real issues of MRP: management and people.
2. Transform what might have been a normal implementation into the installation of a series of computer modules (bills of material, inventory, scheduled receipts, etc).
3. Produce a technically correct piece of software that never becomes a system. Instead of winding up with a structured and effective management system, companies that have embarked on a never-ending search eventually get a set of computer programs that their people will probably never use effectively.

A protracted search also sends mixed messages to the people who will be running MRP II. Your words may say, "People are the most important factor in making MRP II work." Your actions, though, send a different message: "By investing a vast amount of time and man hours in software selection, we really believe software is the key component to getting the system on the air." And with MRP II, mixed messages produce mixed results.

Three other factors also strongly argue against lengthy delays.

1. *Software costs.* Although the list prices of mainframe software has reached an all time high, the Great High Tech Slump of 1985/1986 has turned discounting into a fine art. Also, as MRP II packages become more similar, it has become more difficult to

justify $500,000 and $1 million price tags for mainframe software, especially since fairly complete MRP systems for micro and minicomputers are available in the $10,000 to $50,000 range.

As a result of competition and downward price pressure from microcomputer and minicomputer software vendors, many MRP packages are being discounted by as much as 50 to 60 percent. In a number of instances, vendors have been known to throw in free licenses for additional software (for example, a data base management system required to operate the system) that would normally cost $250,000 or more. Don Nading, a top manufacturing professional at Centrilift Hughes, had an interesting perspective: "After dealing with a few of these companies, I can say with assurance that they've made it clear that they don't discount, but they also don't expect to get the full price for their products anymore."

No one can say for certain that the cost of software will not be less expensive in the future, but can your company afford to wait? Buy now is the message.

2. *The cost of delay.* The return on investment from implementing an effective MRP II system is 200 percent. Even for a Class D user, the return is around 50 percent. Translated into dollars, that means the payback from MRP II in a $60 million company ranges from $25,000 to $100,000 per month—in other words for every month the implementation is delayed, the cost to the company is $25,000 to $100,000. As stated in the Introduction, for many companies the single largest cost during implementation is the cost of delay from an extended software search!

3. *The risk that MRP II will never be implemented.* Any time there is an extended delay in getting MRP II on the air, the likelihood increases that the system will never be fully implemented. Experience suggests a direct correlation between extended implementation schedules with Class C results.

Today, there is no secret to getting the benefits of MRP. But you'll never get to first base if your company is caught up in an eternal search for the perfect package. Act now, save now.

Dream #4:

The more features, the better the package.

Reality #4:

Additional features (beyond the minimum needed for MRP II) are a liability, not an asset.

During the past decade a number of large, complex (and almost always expensive) MRP software systems have been developed. These packages, now considered the second generation of MRP II systems, are often regarded as the "Cadillacs" of MRP software packages. They were created as a response to criticisms that first generation packages were functionally incomplete. The developers of these packages had the right intentions, but may have gone overboard, giving users what amounts to an abundance of solutions to nonexistent problems. (See Figure 1.3 for a listing of typically available but nonessential functions.)

So, what's wrong with having bells and whistles? Isn't more better? Not in the world of software. The idea behind many of the complex second generation systems was that if people didn't want some of the functions included in the package, they would simply turn them off.

Automatic master schedule

Finite loading

Critical ratio/slack time priority calculations

Management priority overrides

Automatic rescheduling

Automatic order release

Sophisticated statistical safety stock computations

Part period balancing, least unit cost, least total cost,
    Wagner Whitin order calculations

Figure 1.3
Typical superfluous functions in commercial software

The problem with that approach is that someone in your company has to know that those functions exist, and has to be able to recognize the symptoms when one of them gets turned on by accident. They also have to know how to turn the function off and recover from any problems that were caused by using the feature. As a result, a tremendous amount of time, energy, and money gets wasted on the training related to functions you don't necessarily want, need, or ever plan to use.

Too many options can also lead to a number of nonproductive meetings about which options to use, and which options not to use. Consider the following situation. A few years ago an MRP software vendor, in response to competition, decided to develop a new master production scheduling module. One of the options it added was forecast consumption logic. Having such logic makes good sense, because as customer orders come in, users need a method for consuming the forecast so that total requirements against the MPS are not overstated. The vendor overstepped the fine line that distinguishes flexibility from complexity, though, and included *six* different ways by which the forecast consumption could be done.

Sounds generous, except that six options mean several or more meetings in which people will debate the merits of each alternative. The meetings will likely consume a significant amount of time, at the end of which the users will have decided that the best logic for their business is not one of the available options, so the package has to be modified anyway.

Moreover, providing six options for forecast consumption actually complicates the effort required to provide the proper logic if it is not part of the system. In this case (as in many cases where there may be some choices in how the logic can be provided), it is generally better if the vendor includes one simple, albeit arbitrary, section of logic and makes it easy to modify. The fact that only a few software vendors take this approach underscores the general lack of articulated design philosophies and guidelines around which new software and upgrades will be developed. And without such guidelines, the tendency is to cover all the bases by including everything but the kitchen sink. (With any luck, a newer third generation MRP II software will be developed and adhere to the design philosophy that, from the user's perspective, simple is beautiful.)

Dream #5:
"State of the art" software has to be the best.

Reality #5:
Too often, the cutting edge turns out to be the bleeding edge.

It's a natural human tendency to want the best— whether it's a suit, a car, or a house. Yet wanting "the best" in MRP II technology can add up to major problems when pursued blindly. Each year The Oliver Wight Companies work with clients that are trying aggressively to implement the tools of MRP II. And each year, some of these clients feel that they must have "state of the art" software, without concern for the lack of Class A or B users who can provide important performance feedback. In many cases, these people feel that state-of-the-art means superior, and proven means out-of-date.

Perhaps "proven" is not as flashy as "state-of-the-art," but there are very good reasons for not being the pioneering user of a software package:

1. The cost of delay. Although you may get MRP II on the air and running successfully, the risk of a software related delay is nearly always higher when the software is unproven. Why risk $100,000 a month or more (the cost of not having an operational MRP II system)?
2. The risk of a false start—having so many software problems that the project is shelved completely for a period of time. Though the benefits from MRP II don't diminish over time, trying to justify MRP II the second time around always seems more difficult and more time consuming.
3. The risk to your credibility with the rest of the organization if things do not work out the way you anticipated. By betting on unproven software, you are betting that the software will not have problems. Yet almost all new MRP II software packages have significant problems, and while the vendor might make every effort to fix them, the software problems may impede your ability to make the behavioral changes needed to get MRP II operating effectively.

In the early 1980s, one group of companies learned about state-of-the-art software the hard way. At that time, a major software company, which had a highly successful data base management system, but no experience with MRP II software, decided to enter the application software business.

With a large and happy group of data base management system users, an excellent marketing organization, and few effective competitors in its market segment, this vendor convinced a number of companies that it was about to release a state-of-the-art MRP II package. Armed with assurances of high levels of support for being among the first users of the system, nearly two dozen project teams convinced their respective managements that the benefits from the ''state-of-the-art'' software offset the risks involved.

In this case, regrettably, nearly everyone misunderstood both the nature and amount of effort required to support over two dozen ''beta test'' sites. Further, no one expected much difference between the support provided for all the users of the data base management system and the support required to implement application software—and yet there turned out to be significant distinctions. A number of sites suffered until the vendor learned what it had to do to support its customers and correct the software problems. Today, on a happier note for the vendor and its customers, most support problems seem to have been resolved and most people implementing the system feel that it is well tested, shaken-down, and backed with appropriate amounts and types of support.

If you do insist on having a ''state-of-the-art'' system, bear in mind a rule of thumb that I first heard from Dave Garwood, president of R. D. Garwood, Inc. and one of the top professionals in my field: when buying unproven software, double the implementation expenses and add at least a year of time to the implementation process. This guideline was proven out several years ago when a defense contractor bought a system that was specially designed to comply with the federal government's ''CSPEC'' reporting requirement. Although there were no Class A users (or Class D users, for that matter) who could be contacted, the company liked the idea of the specialized reporting system, and decided to be a pioneer with the new system. After three years of struggling, the company had had a number of software-related delays, and even contemplated starting from scratch.

The moral? You're better off with yesterday's technology, even if it isn't perfect, than to have today's technology, if it isn't going to work until tomorrow.

Dream #6:
Implementing MRP II means purchasing new software.

Reality #6:
Upgrading existing systems may be an adequate solution.

Many companies today have most of the tools they need to run MRP II. In some cases, they even own MRP software that they have never put on air. In other cases, MRP II might exist as a technical system running on the computer, but the plant is still operated the same way it was before the system was installed. And in still other cases, the companies have a number of MRP subsystems, such as bill of material, inventory, shop order, and purchase order subsystems, and are only missing the planning and scheduling logic of master production scheduling, material requirements planning, and capacity requirements planning.

In any of these situations, replacing the existing systems and subsystems is likely to be a traumatic experience. Besides the burden placed on the systems and data processing departments, the users must learn completely new sets of transactions, reports, screen formats, codes, options, and idiosyncracies. And there is little to be gained from such substitutions in terms of functional benefits.

Take replacing a bill of material processor as an example. In all likelihood, the new bill of material system will not offer anything significantly different from the old one. Yet replacing the system will require people to learn new transactions, reports, etc., so that the company actually loses ground without gaining any tangible benefits. Worse, the approach may lead to costly implementation delays.

For these reasons, the most sensible approach for many larger companies is to upgrade the existing systems, rather than replace them with packaged software. For the company that owns, but has never used, MRP software, implementation or reimplementation might make the most sense. In the case of the company that has all the subsystems to MRP, and only needs the planning logic (master production scheduling, material requirements planning, distribution requirements planning, capacity requirements planning, etc.), contacting a vendor who will sell an interfacing module may be the most effective course of action. (An exception to this rule is the small company, under 500 employees, that has limited systems and subsystems, and would not be disrupted if its people had to relearn an entire package. For such companies, it might make more sense to put in a new system rather than trying to modify or expand the existing programs.)

Even if upgrading does not turn out to be the best decision, it should always be considered as a serious alternative to replacing an entire system.

Dream #7:
The more expensive the package, the better the system.

Reality #7:
Usability of MRP II software has no direct relationship to its cost.

Many software purchasers confuse price with value, which is not surprising in our society today. "You get what you pay for" and "Cheap but costly" are sayings that we've come to accept as self-evident truths. After all, don't the most expensive products offer the most and perform the best? Perhaps when it comes to stereo equipment or European automobiles, but not in the case of MRP II software. In fact, as mentioned before, some of the most complete software available today is designed for microcomputers and minicomputers at a fraction of the cost of mainframe packages.

The utility of MRP II software may even go down with an increase in price. For example, in some cases, high prices are the result of features and options that serve only to increase the complexity and decrease both the ease of use and your ability to do essential modifications.

If you keep in mind the proper goals for the software search, specifically simplicity and basic functionality, pricing differences will probably sort themselves out.

Dream #8:
Elegant systems are essential from Day One.

Reality #8:
In both the long and short term, it's better to go for results first, elegance second.

Your mission, simply stated, is to find software that can be put on air as quickly as possible. Companies that fail to implement MRP in a reasonable time frame often do so because they confuse ends and means—they insist on waiting until every interface is created and every "i" in the documentation is dotted. The Arc Company, for example, delayed implementation an entire year hoping that the whole system would be in final form when they threw the switch. The people responsible for MRP II at this electrical components manufacturer finally realized, however, that they were not only costing their company hundreds of thousands of dollars a month in unrealized benefits, but that they were losing credibility with their management and employees. The educational process had been completed, and everyone knew what he or she had to do to operate MRP II. The only hang-up was that the computer software was not yet in place in its final elegant form.

In a review session on the status of their project, the implementation team discovered the mixed messages it was sending throughout the organization. On the one hand, it was saying, "Software is the least essential part of MRP"; on the other hand, it said, "The impediment to success is technical." Following this revelation, the team quickly put together a three month plan to complete the minimum modifications needed for a pilot run. Some "i's" in the documentation still aren't dotted, but the company quickly achieved high Class B level and may well reach Class A before the ink dries.

Dream #9:
You can implement MRP II without involving the systems and data processing group.

Reality #9:
Systems and data processing people play an important role in implementing effective systems.

Although we have been stressing that MRP is a people-driven process and that focusing on the computing aspects is detrimental, no one can afford to ignore the crucial role that systems and data processing people will play in the overall MRP effort.

Nearly every MRP package requires some upgrades to its functionality, and these will most likely be done by systems and data processing professionals. There's also the issue of interfacing, which is often overlooked. Will you simply turn off the old system on Friday and surprise everyone on Monday? Probably not—the effects would be disastrous. Instead, temporary interfaces will have to be built to tie the new and the old systems together. Who's responsible for those interfaces? Systems and data processing people, of course.

Even after the new system is linked to the old one, some permanent interfaces will eventually have to be built. For example, you will probably want to tie purchasing and payables together. It may be absolutely essential in your company that this interface exists from day one. Or it may be that someone can manually match the two systems until the interfaces are finished. In either case, the data processing effort will not be trivial, and must be estimated and planned for from the beginning.

The only exception may be the very small company that is just getting into computers and systems for the first time. In this case, there are no existing systems that have to be interfaced, either permanently or temporarily. Also, in this kind of small company operating microcomputer systems, it may be possible to purchase fairly complete MRP II software and flexible report writing tools so that what "development" has to be done can be done by users.

As you can see, the process of selecting MRP II software is fraught with perils even before you contact a vendor. But don't be discouraged; every day, companies throughout the world make informed buying decisions and successfully implement MRP. Their success, in large part, is because their people had realistic perspectives that enabled them to anticipate potential problems and pitfalls. As a result, there were fewer surprises—and far fewer opportunities for Murphy's Law to be proven true.

SUMMARY

- There is no such thing as the "perfect" software package. All off-the-shelf software will require some modifications and additions.

- The more time you spend selecting software, the more time you will probably spend implementing your MRP II system. Software selection and evaluation need not exceed months.

- Focus on the basic set of functions required to run MRP. This may be offered in simple packages with fewer options.

- Don't assume that higher priced packages give you more for the money. Corollary: bells and whistles don't make an MRP II system.

- Avoid unproven approaches. The valid testimony for a software package or implementation approach is from its successful users.

- Evaluate your existing system before buying all new subsystems. There's no gain from replacing subsystems that are already in place and working.

- Be realistic about the length of time that will be required for systems and data processing people to create and install interfaces for your system.

Chapter 2

Back to Basics:
What Makes a System Work?

*The future offers us very little hope for those who expect that
our new mechanical slaves will offer us a world in which we
may rest from thinking.*
(Norbert Wiener, mathematician)

Newly armed with a perspective on what off-the-shelf MRP software
can and cannot do, you might be tempted to contact a few vendors and
ask for presentations and proposals. And since we've stressed that it
should only take a few months to make your decision, it might seem
that every minute you spend not talking to vendors cuts into the time
needed to make your selection. Relax. It's premature to get involved
with vendors without first having an understanding why some systems
work and others don't. Once you've gained that understanding, you'll
find it much easier to set the proper goals for the software selection
process, which in turn will minimize the total time you need to spend
evaluating software and implementing MRP II.

In a nutshell, effective systems are those that support human en-
deavors. In business, they help companies become more efficient and
competitive. In transportation, they help guide airplanes safely and
quickly to their destinations. And in manufacturing, effective systems
help managers minimize inventory and produce goods as efficiently as
possible.

All effective systems, whether they are concerned with accounting,
air traffic control, or MRP II, are comprised of several common elements: people, data, and tools (hardware and software). Note the or-

31

der. People are the most important, data is next, and the tools are last.
The fact is, in business, the real power of the computer is its ability to
support people who do basic tasks in massive volumes, particularly
where the volumes are beyond the capabilities of manual systems.

Beyond people, there are four other key factors that determine the
effectiveness of any system: data integrity; the validity of the simulation; timeliness of the results; and the degree to which the system shows
the user how it arrived at a certain result at a certain time (a property
known as "transparency").

In this chapter, we'll look at all the factors that contribute to a working MRP II system. Without such an understanding, someone planning
to implement MRP II or purchase software may confuse the need for
software with some of the other more essential elements of the system.

PEOPLE FACTORS

Understanding

In systems and data processing, the traditional systems development
cycle (i.e. logical design, physical design, programming, testing, implementation, operation) is generally regarded as not being very effective. Most people blame the problem on the amount of time between
"logical design" (user interviews) and implementation. "Unless the
time frame is very short," they say, "the users always change their
requirements." In reality, the problem with the traditional systems development cycle is not that users change their requirements, but that
they probably did not understand their requirements in the first place.
Asking the user "What do you need in a new system?" prior to educating him is likely to elicit a blank response, or the question "What
do *you* think it should have?"

The solution to this problem is not for professional systems and data
processing people to make decisions about what ought to be in a system, but rather to educate the end users about what modern tools are
available for production and inventory management and how they can
be used in his or her areas of the business. This approach makes sense,

because users are the people most likely to understand the problems related to their own jobs. And if they are properly informed about the logic behind the available tools, they can evaluate those tools and implement effective solutions with them.

The need for people to understand the logic of a system is a powerful argument for system simplicity. In fact, unless a feature or a function can be justified on the basis of increased operational effectiveness, it should probably be left out. That's why the "black box" approach is not effective in practice, because often no one (including the system's designer) understands how the system works in all circumstances.

Another argument for simple systems is that people find it difficult to understand how all the different features, options, and codes work together to produce a recommendation or result. Again, as long as people have to be involved, the system's logic needs to be relatively simple.

Ownership

In addition to understanding the logic of the system, people must have a feeling of ownership in it. Ownership is a sense that the system will help them do their job better. Anyone who feels ownership in a system will feel personally responsible for the results it generates. It's the same feeling and satisfaction that an author, artist, or a designer gets from feeling personally committed to his or her work.

Conversely, if the user of the system does not feel ownership, he is likely to think that "it's a data processing system" or "it's a system for the manufacturing department," and no amount of cajoling or exhortation will cause it to produce results—regardless of whether the system has the right logic or accurate data.

A corollary is this: in implementing new systems, the best choice for a project manager is the primary user. For example, when implementing a general ledger system, a person in accounting, not the sales and marketing manager, should be in charge. Likewise, when implementing CAD, a person in engineering, not someone from purchasing, should be responsible for the system. When implementing shop floor control and capacity management, a foreman, not a systems analyst, should oversee the project. And when implementing MRP II, almost anyone, except a staff member from systems or data processing, should be in charge.

Many companies implementing MRP II for the first time fall into one or more of the following traps, each of which creates ownership problems: 1) subcontracting the implementation to consultants; 2) making someone in systems and data processing responsible for getting the system on the air; and 3) assigning the training department the job of educating the users. Each mistake is destined to cause major problems in making the system work even if it eventually goes on the air.

Ownership, at least partially, implies responsibility. In any effective MRP II system, people understand their responsibilities with respect to the data required to operate the system, and what they must do to operate the system. The following are some basic examples of individual responsibilities in operating an MRP II system: in the stock room, only the stock room manager is responsible for the accuracy of the inventory records; in the planning department, a planner takes responsibility for setting lead times, lot sizes, safety stocks, etc.; and in the marketing department, sales people are responsible for a sales plan that will be input into the sales and operations planning process.

During the implementation and operation of an MRP II system, there are numerous ways to promote ownership and define responsibility. One is by means of physical barriers, such as a fence, a gate, and a lock for the stockroom, so that only authorized people may do work in designated areas. A more abstract type of barrier is a security program in the computer so that the software only allows people responsible for certain records to update those records. For example, only stock room people would be allowed to input inventory transactions, only accounting people would be able to update standard costs, only planners would be permitted to update lot sizes, lead times, and safety stocks.

It's also worth noting that psychological barriers can also help define areas of responsibility and ownership. These tend to be unrelated to the software part of the system and may include things as simple as a line on the floor. In one company, a large tool and die manufacturer, the stockroom manager painted a yellow line on the floor, designating his area of responsibility. No one stepped across the line. (Of course it also helped that the stockroom manager was 6' 8'' tall, weighed 290 pounds, and was nicknamed ''Hulk.'') Less imposing would be written company policies, clearly defined procedures, and written job descriptions that clearly define responsibilities. For example, in one Class A company, the stockroom manager's salary increases are tied directly to the inventory record accuracy.

Accountability

Mark Twain once said, ''If you don't like the weather in New England, just wait a minute.'' Perhaps the fickleness of New England's weather makes it hard to predict accurately, but even so, no one really holds the weatherman accountable for a shower that ruins a Sunday picnic. In fact, we've even come to expect that the predictions will be wrong.

That attitude, however, is unacceptable when dealing with a business system. Accountability for results can never be left out, intentionally or by accident. Any time people are removed from the approval process in systems like MRP II, costly mishaps and errors are bound to occur. One manufacturing company, for example, designed a highly automated purchase order system where orders were released automatically and sent to vendors without human review and approval. Imagine the surprise a month after bringing the system on air when ten box cars of toilet paper arrived on a railroad siding near the plant.

In another instance, an automatic purchase order system placed an order to Saudi Arabia for several quarts of a special highly distilled machine oil. Fortunately, in this case, the company got a call from the Saudi capital, asking, ''Do you understand that your order is our entire year's production, and the total cost is $2 billion?''

Many would argue that these kinds of problems can be eliminated from systems by sufficient editing and tests for reasonableness. To some degree this is true. But in the end, someone in purchasing has to be held accountable (when was the last time you fired your computer?), and in that situation, a prudent person will be certain that he has not been engineered out of the approval loop. For the same reason, people are not removed from the approval loop in systems such as the navigational and piloting systems of air and space craft, the monitoring and control systems in nuclear power plants, and the launch systems for our arsenal of ICBMs and B-52s.

In any of these systems, "The computer said to do it" is not and cannot be an acceptable excuse for errors. Nor can it be in a business environment. Consequences are the key to people accepting accountability for the systems they use. And in many cases when designing computer systems, discussions over whether or not certain decisions should be automatic focus on the wrong questions. The real questions are:

1. Does the computer possess the capability to evaluate whether or not taking this action makes sense in all circumstances? And
2. Is the computer capable of determining whether or not the decision can be executed in all circumstances? (I.e. Will people have to be responsible for executing the decision?)

As long as people have to execute decisions, the design of the computer system must not cloud, confuse, or obscure the accountability issues. Figure 2.1 lists certain features that are typically found in MRP II software packages that can cause accountability problems.

In many cases, it is possible to make something more automatic without losing accountability. For example, one feature that has generated a lot of debate in the past is called "automatic rescheduling." In a system with automatic rescheduling, scheduled receipts are auto-

---

1. Automatic master schedule generation.
2. Automatic rescheduling.
3. Automatic order release.
4. Sophisticated ordering rules (part period balancing, least unit cost, etc.).
5. Finite loading logic.
6. Automatic order closure logic.
7. Statistical forecast calculations that lack human review and approval before updating.

Figure 2.1
Features that may cause accountability problems

matically changed to earlier or later dates based on MRP's calculation of the need date.

Although there are some companies where "automatic rescheduling" does work and where scheduled receipt dates are changed automatically by the computer, the system must be set up in a specific way to manage the accountability requirements of the planners and the people in the shop.

In systems where the computer is allowed to change the due date of an order before a planner or the shop people look at the change, the system must produce an exception message indicating the change and people must be held accountable for reviewing these changes. Planners and shop people must review all changed due dates and they must reverse any that are not correct. If someone determines that a reschedule is unrealistic, he must have a method to override the automatic rescheduling logic, and he must make a change to put a realistic due date on the order.

In practice, "automatic" features like automatic rescheduling are not as easy to use or as responsive as they appear on paper. In almost every situation, a plan is being made by the computer and people are responsible for catching any problems and reversing them. This is not only the opposite of the way most people prefer to work, but it is also difficult to hold people accountable for the plan, or for the execution of the plan.

In any system, users *must* have direct operating control over those things for which they will be held accountable. In an extreme example, air traffic controllers may be held responsible for the safety of aircraft, but in a mishap, only the pilot and crew are truly accountable for the results. For this reason, the pilot and the crew have ultimate control over the aircraft.

In an MRP II system, there can be no lip service accountability for a system to work. Consider the following two examples: The Clay Company makes industrial bearings to stock. Each year the sales department is asked to develop a forecast for the coming year. The sales people, however, are never actually held accountable for the results of their forecast, or for achieving the predicted results. In fact, because of certain sales incentives, they intentionally produce a low forecast, which makes them look like heroes when they exceed the predictions.

The low sales forecast, however, doesn't help much with planning for the right material, and manufacturing always seems to be in fire-fighting and expediting mode to keep up with real demands.

At the Smith Company, the pendulum has swung in the opposite direction. Here the sales department always finds itself second-guessing the plant, because at one time the manufacturing arm had a poor track record. To get manufacturing to produce 100,000 units of a particular item, sales generates a forecast of 500,000 units; to get manufacturing to produce 150,000 of the item, sales generates a forecast of 750,000 units. Of course, over the years, manufacturing has discovered that sales always overstates their forecast by a factor of at least five, and they never sell that amount. So manufacturing adjusts all forecast quantities down by a factor of seven. Soon, neither group really knows what the other plans to do, and there is no accountability for the numbers.

In each case, the lack of accountability diminishes the company's productivity and efficiency. At the Clay Company, accountability has been engineered out of the system through the sales incentive program. At the Smith Company, there is general confusion over what sales will be held accountable for, and what manufacturing will be held accountable for. Progress is unlikely until each company realizes that unrealistic forecasts are unacceptable, and that people must be measured by and held accountable for the numbers. In the case of sales, this means the sales plan (of which the forecast is one component); in the case of manufacturing, this means the operations plan (of which an agreed upon rate of output is one component).

The ownership and accountability issues not only affect an operational MRP II system, but come into play as early as the implementation phase. One common mistake in the early stages is to use the "swat team" approach to software selection. This method entails rounding up a crack group of people, and charging them with the duty of finding the best MRP software for the company. The team goes out and finds what it considers to be the best package, recommends it, and is then disbanded as a separate implementation team is formed.

Three months later the implementation team will undoubtedly be having some problems with the software or the software vendor, and they are likely to say, "We would never have selected that package—

it just doesn't answer the problems we need to solve.'' The swat team cannot be held accountable for implementing the system, and without a sense of real ownership on the part of the implementation team, neither can they. For this reason, it is essential that the group charged with software selection is also responsible for bringing the system on the air.

DATA INTEGRITY

Before MRP II and the advent of the computer, the basic inventory numbers in a manufacturing company did not mean very much. In fact, in companies where the real system is staging parts in advance of assembly to identify shortages, there is little reason for accurate inventory records. After all, the parts are going to be physically pulled from stock—what is the real need to maintain an accurate on-hand balance?

Of course, a company must have accurate inventory records in order to have its books certified. But according to the outside auditors, a few extra engines usually cancel out the few short transmissions, so that an inventory accuracy of 42 percent (based on percentage of records accurate within the counting tolerance) turns into 99 percent plus financial accuracy.

And when the real system is knowledgeable employees who have lived through the evolution of the product, where is the incentive to maintain accurate bills of material and routings? Yet, inaccurate data pumped into any computer system will cause invalid results. There is no escaping the old computer adage of ''garbage in, garbage out.'' If your inventory records are close to the national average of inventory accuracy, your boss will inevitably wonder why the company spent all that money on MRP. The same will happen if you feed in bills of material that are 80 percent accurate, or if you load the master schedule to 120 percent of available capacity.

In any system, there are some kinds of data that must be accurate all the time, and others that are less critical. In an MRP II system, the master schedule must be valid, the bills of materials must be 98 percent accurate, and inventory records must be at least 95 percent correct. The accuracy requirements for lead times, lot sizes, safety stocks, and

CATEGORY: HIGH DEGREE OF ACCURACY REQUIRED	GUIDELINE
1. Inventory records	95% or better
On hand balances Scheduled receipts (dates and quantities) Allocations	
2. Bills of material	98% or better
Completeness Structure Quantities	
3. Routings	98% or better
Operations Sequence Work centers	

CATEGORY: MUST PASS THE TEST OF REASONABLENESS	
1. Item planning data	Reasonable and complete
Lot sizes Lead times Safety stocks Shrinkage factors	
2. Bill of material planning data	Reasonable and complete
Scrap factors Product structure lead time offsets	
3. Work center planning data	Reasonable and complete
Work center identification Demonstrated capacity Efficiency Planned queue	
4. Routing planning data	Reasonable and complete
Standards Move time to next operation	

Figure 2.2
Accuracy requirements in an operating MRP II system

forecasts are more forgiving. (See Figure 2.2 for a comparative listing of the accuracy requirements of various MRP II functions.)

Although it is obvious that bad data yield bad results, the lack of data integrity in critical areas is a major problem in many companies. Often, they are not even aware that the problem exists and this is truly unfortunate, since data integrity is the easiest of all the system factors to correct.

SYSTEM FACTORS

Simulation of Reality

Before automating any process, it is critical to ask the question: ''How should it really happen?'' One of the most common mistakes made by anyone getting into systems for the first time is assuming that automating the existing process will produce results. This assumption is risky, because many times the existing formal system (the one that will be automated) is invalid.

For many years, manufacturing companies used a manual order point system based on bin cards containing the available balance for every item in stock. In this system, when the available balance dropped below the order point (a number calculated from the average demand, the lead time, and the desired safety stock), the item was reordered. Because of the relatively simple nature of the bin card system, it was a perfect candidate for computerization.

But while the bin card system and the books of procedures that back it up represented a formal system for many companies, they did not constitute the ''real'' system. The real system was the shortage system that staged parts to identify shortages and then expedited the shortages through the shop to fill the real requirements.

The formal system, in this case the order point system, focused entirely on the ordering of materials—what quantity should be ordered and when it should be ordered. The informal system of staging and expediting tried to answer the real question in manufacturing of ''what do we really need and when do we really need it?'' Few, if any, benefits are to be realized from automating a non-working formal system.

There is enormous payback, however, from using the computer to create a formal system that not only works, but could not be done manually because of the volume or dynamics of the data.

MRP pioneer Oliver Wight once observed: ''The operating systems that work are those where the logic is standard and obvious to the user.'' Whether the system is MRP II, DRP, CAD, air traffic control, or airline reservations, any system that works must be a valid simulation. An airline reservation system, for example, is a valid simulation of the process of manually booking airplane seats by putting boxes on a sheet of paper (each one corresponding to a seat on the plane) and then putting X's into the boxes whenever a seat is sold. That process, in turn, mimics the act of marking each seat that is sold on the airplane itself.

Imagine trying to run a major airline in the 1980s using a manual reservation system! Both the volume of the data and the dynamics of the data would quickly be overwhelming. This is exactly the case in planning and scheduling a manufacturing company. Many small companies have in excess of ten thousand separate item numbers, each of which must be planned and scheduled out beyond their cumulative lead time (often 52 weeks), and each of which is probably dependent upon some other item or items. Tom Wallace gives a tongue-in-cheek estimate that the population of the People's Republic of China and a year's output of #2 lead pencils could not keep up with the calculations of such environments.

The computer was salvation to manufacturing companies once they realized that the real system was not the formal system in the book of procedures, and they began to use the computer to simulate the logic that pulls parts to identify shortages. In doing these projections of shortages, they were able to look ahead months and years, identifying orders that already existed but that needed to be pre-expedited (because they would be needed sooner), and de-expedited (because they were not needed when scheduled) to make available capacity for the orders that were really needed. Later. this system for projecting shortages and planning around them in advance was extended to project shortfalls and overages of capacity, cash flow requirements, tooling needs, etc.

Like the airline reservation system, an MRP II system is a valid simulation that embodies a logic that works independently of the computer or the software. We can therefore speak of a standard logic underlying MRP software, just as we can speak of a standard logic underlying all double entry accounting systems. Some companies balk at this idea, saying, "We're unique, we're different—a standard logic can't apply to us. Our customers are the most demanding . . . our vendors are the most unreliable . . . our manufacturing is the most complex . . . we're made-to-stock . . . we're made-to-order . . . we're big . . . we're small," and so on.

Such arguments do not hold up against the experience of MRP users during the past 20 years. Today, we have a body of knowledge that can be successfully applied to "unique" problems. Thousands of companies have learned that the fundamental tools and approaches for planning and scheduling can be the same whether the factory makes brassieres or jet engines. And while the specific techniques differ among effective MRP users, just as their charts of accounts will differ, the message is clear: there *is* a standard logic that works.

In manufacturing, the logic that forms the basis for effective planning and scheduling includes both standard functions and standard human engineering. As we will see in Chapters 5 and 6, referencing the standard logic is an essential part of selecting and evaluating an MRP II software package.

Timeliness

In addition to being a valid simulation, a system can be effective only if it performs the simulation within a usable time frame. Take a weather forecasting system as an example. A weather forecasting system would be of little value if it took more than 24 hours to generate tomorrow's forecast. Similarly, an air traffic control system that was not updated in real time would have serious problems dealing with typical peak loads at a major airport.

In manufacturing, experience suggests that an inventory system where the records are updated less frequently than once a day is of little value. Experience also suggests that the material requirements plan must be updated at least once per week (many companies are updating the plan

TYPE OF DATA OR INFOR-MATION	MAXIMUM TIME BE-TWEEN UPDATE RUNS	DESIRABLE

Basic foundational data
  Inventory records
  Scheduled receipts
  Bills of material
  Routings
  Item and work center info
  Shop feedback
	Daily	On-line

Sales and operations plan	Monthly	Weekly/monthly
Forecast update	Weekly	Daily

Master production schedule
  MPS quantities/dates
  Report
  Available to promise
	
	Daily
	Weekly
	Daily
		
		On-line
		Daily
		On-line

Material requirements plan	Weekly	Daily or more frequently
Capacity requirements plan	Every other week	Weekly, more frequently for simulations
Dispatch list	Daily	Beginning of each shift or more frequently
Vendor schedule	Weekly	Daily or more frequently (electronic data interchange)
Input/output control report	Weekly	Daily

Figure 2.3
Updating frequency for various data and information

daily, and some do so continuously in real time). Figure 2.3 shows the recommended updating frequency for various types of data in an MRP II system.

Transparency

Conceivably, you could have a system that has the right logic and produces timely results, but is of limited use because it lacks "transparency" or "system visibility." Transparency gives the user the ability to look into the system and answer the question: "Why did it generate that number this time?"

Being able to understand how any system arrived at a certain result is critical, because inevitably there will be situations in which you cannot do what the system recommends. If that happens, an effective system must: 1) provide a way to understand why the recommendation was made; 2) rely on a human to evaluate the situation, make a decision, and implement a different solution; and 3) check for any problems with the solution and identify them to the human operator.

Unless a system is transparent, there will likely be problems with accountability. As an example, in MRP II, a common recommendation is an exception message saying, "Reschedule this order to an earlier date." If the planners cannot determine why it is telling them to reschedule the order, and they cannot comply with the recommendation, how can they be held accountable for hitting the schedules from MRP?

One solution is called "pegging," which is a specific feature designed to make an MRP system transparent. Pegging enables a user to track down or "peg" the source of a requirement back to the parent manufacturing order, customer order, or forecast that caused it. (See Figure 2.4 for a list of other features that contribute to the transparency of an MRP system.)

Consider how pegging greatly facilitates the work of a planner. A planner's job essentially amounts to matching supply and demand; that

---

1. Pegging of gross requirements and allocations
2. Transaction history
3. Time phased MRP displays that include all descriptive information that affects the exception messages and planned orders, the time phased picture, pegging, details to scheduled receipts and firm planned orders, exception messages
4. Capacity requirements pegging
5. Scheduled receipts status displays
6. Detail pegging reports for projected inventory valuations, cash flow projections

Figure 2.4
Features that promote transparency

is, he or she must make the supply for an item match the demand for that item. In most situations, this is done by rescheduling shop orders or purchase orders to earlier or to later dates. Inevitably there are situations, however, in which the planner cannot reschedule an order to an earlier date. In that case, the planner must still do his or her job of matching supply and demand, only this time by changing the demand to match the fixed supply.

Pegging provides a way for the planner to trace the source of the demand back to customer orders, forecast requirements, a higher level manufacturing schedule, a distribution order, or perhaps an inter-plant order. The ability to peg the source gives the planner an insight into the source of the demand and the reason for the rescheduling recommendation, which in turn gives him or her a better sense of how to respond. In this way, the planner can quickly and intelligently resolve the problem in the schedule.

Without pegging, finding the source of a requirement is much more difficult. Although a planner could search through the where-used listings from the bill of material system and review every parent item, from a practical point of view that would mean searching through piles of paper and possibly hundreds of items, many of which would be inactive. That, of course, consumes enormous amounts of valuable time and energy. In some big volume situations, this kind of search is simply impossible without pegging. And in such cases, the problem may go unresolved, so that people will be working to schedules that are invalid (the matching sets of components are not required if the item is not going to be available). In addition, there could be a shortage when the parent manufacturing schedule was actually released, and inventory would be higher than needed (all the other matching components would be available but it won't be possible to assemble and ship the product).

As you can see, transparency is a vital aspect of an effective system. The need for transparency is perhaps best summed up by Oliver Wight, who pointed out that "unless accountability for decisions and their execution can be transferred entirely to the computer, they have to be made by people." In an ideal world, the system would have all possible logic to handle every conceivable situation. But until we reach such a utopian state, systems must provide ways for people to understand the logic and pinpoint the source of its recommendations.

As a parting thought on the transparency issue, and a marvelous comment on the need to be able to see into the visible logic of a system, consider a scene from the best-selling book *The Hitchhiker's Guide to the Universe*, in which the most powerful, sophisticated computer in the universe, Deep Thought, is asked to determine the great Question of Life, The Universe, and Everything. After hundreds of thousands of years of processing, Deep Thought spit out the answer: "42." When asked how it achieved that answer, Deep Thought responded, "I checked it very thoroughly . . . and that quite definitely is the answer. I think the problem, to be honest with you, is that you've never actually known what the question is."

SUMMARY

- Understanding is prerequisite to ownership and accountability. All are essential to making a system work.
- The quality of data has a major impact on the quality of any system's output.
- An effective system is a valid simulation of a particular process; that is, it has the proper logic. MRP II has a logic that correctly simulates the processes that occur in the manufacturing environment.
- Timely updating of data is a prerequisite to an effective system.
- Effective systems are transparent; they make their logic obvious to the user.

Chapter 3

The Software Selection Game:

Rules for Success

Winning isn't everything. It's the only thing.
(Vince Lombardi, football coach)

If you were to ask most people what they want to get out of their MRP II software search, they would probably be puzzled by the question; isn't that somewhat like asking, "Who's buried in Grant's tomb?" Not at all. While the overall goal of the search is to find software that will enable your company to operate an MRP II system, there are a number of issues that must be resolved as part of the decision—for example, the issues of the modifications that will have to be made, the interfaces that will have to be built, and determining who will make them are all critical concerns. Such considerations are significant: an MRP package that will take five years to interface to your existing financial systems will be of little value, even if it seems excellent from other perspectives.

There is also the question of the utility or value received. How do you measure utility? If you do not have a method for making such a determination in advance, you will have difficulty comparing two packages side-by-side when they offer different configurations of functions, features, options, codes, and capabilities at vastly different prices.

Finally, how will you make sure that what you see is what you really get? If you don't identify functions that can be specifically identified and bound into a contract, you may find yourself with a very expensive but useless mass of code. Understanding the basic objectives of the software evaluation process is essential to avoiding delay. Experience suggests that many of the problems in the process and in the installation phase can be avoided if everyone associated with the project would understand and agree to four basic objectives:

Objective 1:
To find a workable MRP II software package.

Too often people get caught up in defending their favorite package. Factions may develop, and everyone will forget that the objective is to come up with a workable program now rather than the best package after a five year search. Both before and after the actual selection, it is generally better not to tout the virtues of the software. After all, assuming that the software has the basic functionality of MRP II or can be modified to provide it (within the implementation time frame), the software is the "C" item in MRP II success. In short, be content with simply getting people to agree that the package will serve the needs of the company and that they will hold up their end of the bargain in using it.

The dangers of letting personal preferences and biases guide the selection process is well illustrated by the experience of the Arnold Company, a heavy equipment manufacturer who had previous experience operating Class A MRP II at three facilities, and decided to implement a fourth. At that time, it also had to decide whether it should modify its existing software or buy a new package. The "analysis" quickly turned into a heated brawl fueled by emotion rather than objective thinking. As a result, MRP II became a political football between two factions warring for turf, and the selection process was delayed by more than a year. Both sides had clearly lost sight of the objective of finding a working MRP system in the shortest possible time. The sad part, of course, is that although one faction was the "winner" (the group seeking new software), the company was ultimately the loser, in terms of valuable lost time and money.

Objective 2:
To identify modifications that will compensate for missing functionality and the points of interface to existing systems.

We have already emphasized the fact that no package will be complete, and that some degree of modification and customization will be necessary. Your goal is to determine what changes and/or additions have to be made, and who is going to carry them out. That also means determining whether it is feasible for you to do the work yourself, or whether you will contract with the vendor to do it, or whether you need to find additional third party resources. In any case, you must find out how much it will cost, and when it can be done. These questions should be answered by a specific schedule and/or resource plan. Again, any delays caused by scheduling will ultimately cost significant amounts in unrealized MRP benefits.

The idea is not to write detailed specifications for how a particular problem will be resolved, but to identify surprises that would otherwise occur at exactly the wrong time, in the middle of the implementation. Having identified such potential surprises, a plan can be laid out to eliminate them.

Though a few companies underestimate the effort that modifications require (and as a result wind up delaying their implementation by many months), more often companies are surprised that a modification has to be made at all. And in instance after instance, the need for the modification is found at the point that the particular function is going to be used.

The Trainer Machine Tool Company, for example, bought a very popular MRP software package after conducting a fairly thorough analysis. No one, however, thought to check the mechanics of final assembly scheduling provided in the package, or to plan for the needed modifications. And, although the users decided exactly how they wanted to do final assembly scheduling during their education sessions, they had not progressed far enough into the software installation at that point to conduct training sessions using their software. As a result, no one verified that the final assembly scheduling approach they had selected would in fact work with the software. In effect, several minor failures in the evaluation and education process added up to one big problem when they found themselves within one month of running their pilot with a package that did not have the specific features they would need for the final assembly scheduling task.

Under normal circumstances, the lack of final assembly scheduling software at Trainer probably wouldn't have caused a crisis. Had the problem been identified in advance, a plan to develop final assembly scheduling software would have been in place, and enough lead time (perhaps three to six weeks of effort) would have been provided to resolve the difficulty. In this case, however, the company had got right up to the point of throwing the switch with little time for recovery, the systems and data processing resources were being used on other essential changes and improvements and couldn't be deployed rapidly, and the confusion caused a six month delay in implementation.

The moral is clear: Know what you are going to need ahead of time. But there is another important lesson here, too: people just cannot drop everything at the last minute because you discover that your software is missing necessary functions. Avoid disaster by being prepared.

Objective 3:

To judge software alternatives fairly and on the basis of cost versus utility.

This goal often seems difficult to meet, because two contending packages may have different degrees of features, functions, options, etc. and vastly different costs. Wouldn't this be like comparing apples and oranges? Not if you base your comparison on their respective costs of delay, and ask, "How much will it cost to bring each one up to the functionality of a standard MRP II system?" The real cost of software is:

Package price + modification costs + cost of delay

Understanding how to analyze the cost of software can save you tens of thousands of dollars, or more. For example, several years ago a number of companies were struggling to compare one MRP package that sold for approximately $250,000 ($150,000 for the software, $100,000 for support) against another package that sold for $60,000 ($50,000 for the software and $10,000 for support). True, the lower cost program was a regenerative MRP system while the more expensive one was a net change MRP package—but this difference was hardly enough to justify the difference in price. And when companies performed detailed evaluations, they found that the less expensive package actually offered more advanced financial functions.

In fact, in most situations where the two packages were compared against the standard logic of MRP II, and evaluated in terms of missing functionality and the associated costs of delays in creating the desired features, companies concluded that the contenders had *about the same degree of utility*!

What accounted for the enormous discrepancy in price? Some said the cheaper package was underpriced, while others pointed to the more expensive package as being overpriced. The vendor of the less expensive package had an interesting perspective on the situation, though; according to its technical vice president, "Software prices are probably already too high—they will go up for a short time more, but eventually they will come down."

In fact, the list price on the $250,000 package did eventually fall to $110,000. As the example shows, however, you may not have to wait for drastic price reductions—everything you need might be found in a lower priced package that gives you as much or more value.

Objective 4:
To negotiate a mutually acceptable contract.

Once you have identified what functionality exists in the system and works properly, what is missing from a package and how it will be fixed, the next step is to turn the evaluation documents and plans into a contract. Therefore, once you finish evaluating a piece of software, you want to incorporate in the contract language stating that the functions work in accordance with the standard logic for planning and scheduling, and that specific missing components will be added.

Some might object, saying in effect, ''It isn't fair to the software vendor to surprise him at the end by changing the rules. After all, he is offering a product that conforms to documentation that you've had a chance to review.'' The fact of the matter is that you shouldn't be surprising the vendor at all—you've said from the beginning that you wanted to buy a system capable of MRP II. He proposed something, and participated in the evaluation to determine whether it does match the standard logic for planning and scheduling. There should be no surprise at the end, and the vendor should be more than willing to specify which tools the system actually includes, and which it doesn't—and do it in writing. Writing down which tools are part of the system provides as much protection to the software supplier as it does to you the purchaser.

Finally, in situations where a vendor has represented that a feature or function is not part of the software but will be in some future release, it is important that such intentions be specified in the contract. This kind of situation might also call for a performance penalty as additional protection. The details of performance penalties and other contractual points are explained in depth in Chapter 7.

The need to protect yourself with a sound contract, as the Electron Components Company discovered, can help eliminate hassles caused by honest misunderstandings. Electron was in the process of investigating MRP packages just as IBM announced a new disk drive technology, fixed block architecture, and wanted software that would be compatible with the new storage system. ''No problem,'' said the salesperson who represented a package highest on the Electron list. He even agreed to amend the standard contract by stating that the software had to be compatible with the new technology. Electron signed the modified contract, as did the branch office management of the software company just before passing the contract ''upstairs'' for corporate technical review. Shortly afterwards the salesperson got a phone call from the corporate technical group saying that the software wasn't currently compatible, and might not be compatible for at least a year, and "would the client company consider an alternative [using the older technology] until then?"

As a result of the provision in the contract, Electron was able to get out of a contract for a $400,000 piece of software that it could not use. True, it would have been able to recover its money through negotiation or legal means, but who wants to tie up nearly half a million dollars, let alone go through the time, expense, and aggravation of this kind of effort?

Another company, Painter Inc., was also saved from implementation problems by good contract provisions. This firm already had a large investment in one brand of computer, and wanted MRP software that would run on it. A software selection team narrowed the list from 20 to five vendors, and went through a fairly normal evaluation process with one exception; they chose *not* to meet with the vendors to discuss and evaluate the logic of the system in detail. Instead, they relied on answers to a questionnaire that specified individual functions that would be part of a standard MRP system, and a demonstration of the system done by the vendor's marketing department. When they finally chose a system, they fortunately got the vendor to agree in the contract that the package included all of the functions of *The MRP II Standard System* (a research report published by Oliver Wight Software Research), except for those explicitly identified as missing. Moreover, the vendor agreed that the company would be given a trial period during which it could install the software and run it through a series of acceptance tests where they checked the logic against *The Standard System*. All they asked in return was a short period in which to respond to any functional problems turned up in the software acceptance testing.

When Painter used the software, it not only discovered that it did not conform to the functions of the Standard System, but it was also loaded with bugs and problems of conforming to its own documentation. Over a period of several weeks the company and the vendor held a series of meetings to identify what the problems were, and the vendor, who had been marketing the software as an MRP II package, realized that the software did not do MRP in any modern sense—it was really designed as a job tracking system for small manufacturers who were not involved in planning and scheduling.

Because of the contract clauses agreed to at the start, each company understood its responsibilities under the agreement. The software company made an honest effort to correct the problems—and Painter made a sincere attempt to work with them to try to salvage the situation. In the end, though, there was simply too much work to be done—but because of an agreed upon and reasonable contract protecting both parties, Painter and its initial software vendor parted company on friendly terms and before the software problems had a chance to affect the implementation.

GUIDELINES FOR ACHIEVING THE SELECTION GOALS

1. NEVER MAKE A SOFTWARE DECISION UNTIL INITIAL EDUCATION IS COMPLETE.

One of the bigger mistakes a company getting into MRP II for the first time can make is to begin looking at software before completing its initial education; the biggest mistake is making the actual decision on software before the initial education. People who have not been through the educational process before looking at software have more questions about what is meat and what is fat, and typically end up making less well informed, less effective buying decisions—and taking longer to do it.

In the end, of course, the real issue is not how fast any buying decision is made—if it were, you could flip a coin—but rather whether an informed decision was made in the fastest period of time.

Many problems in evaluating MRP II software stem from a combination of the lack of user education and the manner in which software is often presented. Too often, considerable time is spent reviewing features and options in the software that have not been proven in practice, or which are not applicable to the prospective client company's specific situation. In this situation, the lack of understanding of MRP II generates confusion, because people begin to debate whether these features and options are essential to making the system work. Confusion leads to a lengthier selection process, which in turn results in costly implementation delays.

Some readers might object to this point, saying that "you are simply taking a long process [software selection] and replacing it with an equally long process [education] prior to the software decision." There are two reasons this isn't the case. One is that the educational process simply should not drag on longer than necessary and has to be done anyway. Second, although the educational process will not cut the evaluation and selection process from 18 months to zero, it will significantly shorten the overall time and improve the quality of the decision because the users are better informed.

Sadly, software selection is one of the toughest things to defer, because everyone "knows" that to make MRP work, you must have software. If upper management is chomping at the bit, however, it is possible to do some limited selection work in advance. For example, you might develop a short list prior to education, strictly on the basis of technical capabilities. If you are not pressed to forge ahead, though, experience suggests that you are best off waiting until everyone has been educated.

2. GET YOUR BUDGET APPROVAL BEFORE YOU LEAP.

In most companies, getting approval for money to buy MRP II software is not difficult. After all, even the general manager who imagines MRP II to be

1. A glorified form of Pac Man;
2. Something they are going to do down in the data processing department to fix these damn shortages and missed shipments;
3. Some program they cooked up out in the factory

also knows that MRP II requires a computer, and computers obviously require software, and software is expensive. No problem convincing this kind of general manager that a software purchase of $300,000, $500,000, or more is valid—but you are asking for trouble if you have not figured out your bottom line prior to signing on the software vendor's dotted line.

Imagine yourself as project manager in the following three-part drama:

Truth and Consequences

ACT I

The Time: Three months after signing the software contract.

Your Discovery: The inventory records that your accounting firm said are 99 percent accurate are really only 99 percent accurate in net dollars (the two extra transmissions cancel out the missing engine) and the physical accuracy of the records is really 42 percent.

The Setting: The general manager's office as you try to explain the situation.

The Conversation:

PROJECT MANAGER: "Gee boss, I don't know how we could have overlooked this—everyone just assumed that when the auditors said our inventory records were accurate, and when we put it in our annual report to our stockholders . . . Maybe it explains why we have so many shortages around here, though. And just maybe it's the reason we seem to average a new controller here every four years—you know what they say up at corporate, if there's an inventory shrink, fire the controller. In any case though, it's a small error. We figure that about $150,000 should be enough to lock up the stockroom, buy some counting scales, calculators, etc.—and really fix this accuracy problem so MRP will work."

GENERAL MANAGER (a bright, understanding, rational and enlightened individual who has taken the time to read that little book on MRP that you gave him): "I can understand how someone can make a mistake like that. And I remember from that little book on MPR III that you gave me how important the inventory balance is to the calculation—how if the starting number is wrong, you'll end up with the wrong exception messages and planned orders. And we'd better get this problem fixed now, so I'll see that you get the money out of current earnings."

ACT **II**

The Time: Three months after finding out about the inventory records.

Your Latest Discovery: The bills of material, which everyone felt were "pretty good," are at best "pretty bad." A number of bills of material exist with "as required" quantities, and others do not have the right components based on the way the people on the floor are building the product today. In addition, someone in the stockroom mentioned that in the casting area, the same part number was being used to identify raw castings and machined painted castings.

The Setting: The hall outside the General Manager's office as you try to explain the situation.

The Conversation:

PROJECT MANAGER (nervously): "Gee boss, I don't know how we could have overlooked this—everyone agreed that the bills of material were in pretty good shape—just a few minor things that had to be adjusted. But when we got the engineers, foremen, purchasing people, stockroom guys, and cost accountants in the same room to resolve some of these problems . . . Maybe it explains why we have so many variances in our cost accounting system. And just maybe the reason we've had problems seeing the benefits from the new million dollar CAD system we bought. In any case though, it's a small error. We figure that about $90,000 should be enough to put several people on the job full time—we can have this problem licked with about a year's effort."

GENERAL MANAGER (a bright, understanding, rational and enlightened individual who has taken the time to read that little book on MRP that you gave him, but who seems a little less patient today than you've seen him before): "I can understand how you could make a mistake like that. And I remember from that little book on MPP IV that you gave me how important the bills of material are to the calculation—how the bill of material is the scheduling network for MPP IV, how if you start with the wrong scheduling network at the top of the product structure, you'll end up with the wrong exception messages and planned orders, and you'll make or buy the wrong things. And we'd better get this problem fixed now, so I'll see that money is transferred from the CAD project to the MPP budget so you can get right on it.''

ACT III

The Time: Three months after finding out about the bill of material problem.

Your Latest Discovery: People make systems work. No one really understands how MRP II will work in the company. They do know what transactions exist in the software and how to use them, but no one can agree on how the sales and operating plan will be developed, what the guidelines are for managing the master production schedule, or how engineering changes will be implemented. You've concluded that the only solution is a company-wide education program stressing the principles of MRP and working through the details of how the company will be managed using MRP II.

The Setting: The lobby around quitting time as you catch the General Manager for the first time in several months.

The Conversation:

PROJECT MANAGER (very nervously): "Gee boss, I'm glad to be able to catch you—I tried making an appointment but Wanda said your calendar was full. We have a small problem with our MRP II implementation—I don't know how we could have overlooked this" (stammering now), "everyone agreed that they knew how MRP worked, and, and, and we have a lot of APICS fellows, but we seem to have some problems in agreeing on how we are going to-to-to manage using the new tools MRP II provides. It's a small, uh small, well fairly small problem though. We figure that about, uh, $150,000 should be enough to do an effective education program. You know—a combination of outside classes and in house sessions using video. It will help us get back on track—we hope to make up some of the delays we've had and should be able to finish up only 14 months late.''

GENERAL MANAGER (a bright, formerly understanding, rational and enlightened individual who had taken the time to read that little book on MRP that you gave him, but who everyone agrees seems to have changed recently, becoming red-faced and impatient each time the subject of MRP II comes up): "Gee, I understand exactly how you made that mistake. And I know exactly how to fund part of this program. Please stop off in the janitor's office in the morning—there'll be a mop waiting for you."

Of course, this is an extreme and unrealistic situation—not because these kinds of mistakes don't happen, but because most project managers do not have the courage or ego strength to go back to executive management and say that they've made blunders of such magnitude. In fact, companies that make these mistakes limp along getting few of the benefits from MRP. Five years later—which is about the time it takes to purge the memory of a failed implementation—someone else may come along and pick up the threads. The lesson is that you must do your cost benefit analysis and have your justification worked out well before you code your first transaction.

3. GIVE THE SELECTION/IMPLEMENTATION TEAM SOME MUSCLE.

We have already discussed the major drawbacks of the "swat" team approach to MRP software selection, and the importance of letting those who select the software be responsible for implementing it. Assuming that the software selectors will also be the software implementors, what level of personnel should they be? Some companies make the mistake of only including people below the managerial or supervisory level. This usually fails because MRP is primarily a behavioral change within an organization, and numerous management studies have determined that the only people capable of effecting deep-seated change are those who are perceived as leaders. Junior data clerks and administrative assistants simply do not have the clout to bring about the needed changes in attitude and operating style.

Ideally, an MRP implementation team will have a full-time project manager, one or two systems people, and various department managers serving in a part-time capacity. The individual department managers would delegate a fair amount of responsibility, and would also do the inside teaching. For a complete discussion of the make-up of MRP teams, see *MRP II: Making It Happen* by Tom Wallace (Appendix B).

4. LET DP COORDINATE THE EVALUATION EFFORT.

While the data processing department should not have responsibility for selecting the software, systems and DP staff is often responsible for contacting vendors, coordinating presentations, vendor visits, etc., and should have a veto vote based on package technology. If the company already has a computer, operating system, data base management software, etc., the systems and data processing department should be able to demand that MRP software is compatible with it. Also, since many companies feel most comfortable having DP make the initial contact with software vendors, DP also has the added responsibility of reducing the universe of possible suppliers.

5. DON'T BITE OFF MORE THAN YOU CAN CHEW.

As we discussed in Chapter 1, it is best to avoid the tendency of starting off with the most elegant possible system. While it would be gratifying to have all possible interfaces and modules in place, only focus on those that are essential. This keeps the burden on DP and other departments at a minimum.

6. FIND THE MIDDLE GROUND.

Many software designers assume that companies are willing to toss out their existing subsystems (bills of material, inventory, and scheduled receipts), even if they work. In a large company, though, getting rid of working systems is a traumatic experience that requires the re-education of all users, and may delay the benefits of using MRP. Besides, every company has "pockets of excellence"—subsystems that function extremely well. It may be a master schedule, a forecasting system, or an engineering change control system. In any case, see what you can salvage before investing in a totally new system.

The opposite approach, "Let's make the present system work," is the belief that all you have to do to achieve MRP II results is to "motivate the troops." In truth, no amount of motivation can compensate for an invalid simulation. If your formal system has the wrong logic, the only alternative is to replace it.

Whichever path you wind up taking, start off from a mid-ground position; if you are convinced from the start that one approach is the correct one, you may wind up making a poor decision. Remember your overriding concern: to get an *effective* MRP II system in a minimum of time, either by modifying existing systems or bringing a new package on air.

7. BEWARE THE "HYPER-DOCUMENTATION SYNDROME."

If there is a black hole for MRP implementations, it is the need to document every system in a company. And if you delay implementing MRP until everything is documented, you could delay its enormous benefits for years. While you certainly do need to evaluate your existing systems to see which portions, if any, can be used, how do you do so without becoming afflicted with hyper-documentation syndrome?

The solution is to use an agreed upon standard for MRP II as the basis for any software analysis. The question then becomes, "Here's the standard for MRP II—how do we achieve each of these functions? Does our existing system match up? If not, how can we modify it? What outside software packages would fit the bill? By taking this approach you have the best chance of assessing your needs with a minimum of documentation.

8. UNDERSTAND THE DIFFERENT SOFTWARE SOURCES.

MRP software can be obtained from three sources: software suppliers, hardware manufacturers, and your own data processing department. The first two categories have advantages and disadvantages. The third category has significant problems when the software is being developed from scratch, but may be an excellent alternative when there are already a number of working systems in place and all that remains is upgrading a few selected "modules." Figure 3.1 provides an overview of each source.

SOURCE: HARDWARE MANUFACTURER

Advantages:

1. The software will run on your computer
2. Better accountability
3. Price

Disadvantages:

1. Not primary business
2. No incentive to reduce hardware resources
3. More tied to vendors' proprietary products

Neutral:

1. Support locations

SOURCE: SOFTWARE SUPPLIER

Advantages:

1. Primary business
2. Some incentive to reduce hardware resources required
3. Higher degree of independence
4. Longer term maintenance

Disadvantages:

1. Financially small
2. Price

Neutral:

1. Support locations

SOURCE: HOMEGROWN FROM SCRATCH

Disadvantages:

1. Time required
2. Design the tool syndrome
3. Designed around today's business conditions

Figure 3.1
Sources for MRP II software

Hardware Vendors

The major hardware vendors—IBM, Honeywell, Sperry Univac, NCR, Hewlett-Packard—are the most well-known suppliers of software. Most of them offer software designed to run on their own systems.

Advantages:

1. The software is guaranteed to run on the vendor's equipment.
2. The same vendor is accountable for both hardware and software.
3. The price of the software may be significantly lower than software from other sources. In many cases, the ultimate cost of the software is less too.

Disadvantages:

1. Hardware vendors are in the business of building and selling computers. Since MRP software is never going to be a major part of their revenue stream, they may put less effort into enhancing or improving it, especially in lean times.
2. A hardware manufacturer in general has little incentive to reduce the resources needed to run its software, such as memory, or to make the software more efficient.
3. The software may be tied to a particular type of computer or data base management system. As a result, moving from one computer or data base to another may require significant modifications to the MRP system.

Neutral:

1. Support locations. A major hardware vendor will certainly have specialists on staff who know your package. The offset, though, is that even if the vendor has an office down the street from your plant, the people who are knowledgeable about MRP software probably will not be there. So you will most likely end up doing business with someone out of town, especially if you need technical assistance.

Software Vendors

The number of MRP software vendors has grown from a handful to more than 150 over the past 15 years. In addition to striving for excellent software, many also offer on site consulting, support, and training in conjunction with their programs. In some cases these extra services can be extremely valuable.

Advantages:

1. Software is generally the vendor's primary product, so the package may have more features, offer more functionality, or have better human engineering than those packages offered by hardware vendors.
2. The vendor has an incentive to reduce hardware requirements, since his market increases if more computers can run his software.
3. You may have a higher degree of independence. In some cases, you will be able to run the packaged software on more than one type of hardware, which gives you the flexibility to change computers in the future without incurring the trauma of changing working systems in the user departments. An example of software like this would be the systems written for the UNIX operating system—UNIX (or one of its derivatives like XENIX) runs on over 40 different types and sizes of computer equipment.

   Sometimes, you can buy software that is independent of data base management system software. This type of system provides flexibility to change data base management systems later without having to change the application software—all you have to do is unload the data base, replace the interface module for the data base management system, and reload.

   At least that's the way data base independent MRP II software is supposed to work. And in situations where a company actually has a working data base management system (DBMS) and switches to another, data base independent MRP II software is the most sensible and fastest way to make the change. Regrettably, I see few companies that are actually making such a change. And in situations where a company doesn't change its DBMS, but where they bought this type of software, they may be paying for increased flexibility through higher license fees (it costs more to develop this type of software) and loss of throughput (data base independence may have been achieved at the expense of performance).
4. Software vendors generally provide longer term maintenance for their products. This is not to say that a vendor will likely support the product for 20 years; nevertheless, in general the support is likely to be available longer than the support offered by hardware vendors.

Disadvantages:

1. Software suppliers are significantly smaller than hardware vendors, and may run out of support capacity if the package becomes very popular.
2. The price is usually much greater than the price of software purchased through hardware vendors.

Neutral:

1. Support locations. Support will generally come from a central location, just as it would for hardware manufacturers selling MRP II software.

In-House Development

After looking at various MRP packages from software and hardware vendors and determining the effort required to interface them to existing systems, some companies may be tempted to write the software themselves. Writing software may be a more sensible idea than purchasing a package in either of the following situations:

1. Many, or most, of the subsystems that make up an MRP II system are already in place, and where the development effort is mostly upgrading these existing systems.
2. There are only a few modules missing from the existing system. For example, the existing system lacks a master production scheduling system and capacity requirements planning, but all the other functions of MRP II are in place.

On the other hand, having no software and writing an MRP II system from scratch is a bad idea. True, a few pioneers did successfully write their own systems, but the overall track record for home-grown MRP II software written from scratch is poor. Listed below are the disadvantages associated with developing MRP II software from scratch:

Disadvantages:

1. Time involved. Part of the problem is that MRP II software is large by software standards. Many commercial packages have in excess of 1,000,000 lines of COBOL code and the equivalent of 50 or

more years of development effort before being released. Not surprisingly, those users who have succeeded in writing their own MRP software have spent a great deal of time developing the system. And in most cases, the cost of delaying MRP far exceeds any savings realized by using in-house resources.

2. The Design the Tool Syndrome. Another problem with home-grown MRP software is what has been called the "design the tool" syndrome, in which a company spends an enormous amount of energy creating a system, only to find that it is still designing it long after the time it could have taken to implement a commercially available product. The difficulty is that people who design their own software tend to develop custom systems, and must therefore rediscover all the mistakes that MRP software vendors and users have collectively made during the past 25 years.

3. Who wants to test it? When Boeing chooses to release its first airplane without wings, you will probably not find me on the maiden voyage. I feel the same way about unproven MRP II software—even though manufacturing companies don't crash and burn, the pain from an implementation failure is just as excruciating.

4. Finally, home-grown MRP software tends to be designed around current business decisions. For example, a company may not have distribution centers or branch warehouses when the MRP system is written. As a result, the program would be designed without the capacity to support distribution centers. The following year, if the company wants to introduce distribution centers, it would have to go back to the drawing board and design an appropriate system. And while the software is being developed, the distribution center will function without the advantages of MRP.

To sum up the problems with home-grown MRP software when it is written from scratch:

1. The time required to develop it generally exceeds the implementation time frame.
2. The implementation itself is stretched out, thereby delaying the payback from MRP.
3. There are none who've blazed a trail with the software.
4. Errors of the past must be discovered first hand.

The chapters that follow provide the tools for a company to evaluate any MRP II software, whether it is a package from a hardware or software vendor, or an existing system that is already running in the company. By observing the principles explained in Chapters 4-7, you can improve your chances of successfully making an informed software decision in the shortest possible time.

SUMMARY

- The ultimate goal of the MRP software selection process is to select the least traumatic software approach, whether totally new or made up of existing systems, and to implement it as quickly as possible. That means focus on finding a *workable* MRP system, not the ideal MRP system.
- Identifying what modifications have to be made, and who will do them, is a key goal of the selection process.
- MRP packages with different functionality can be fairly evaluated by determining how long it will take to create the missing features.
- Once the specifications for an MRP package are determined, each point should be carefully folded in a contract.
- Make sure that your educational process is complete and your budget is approved before moving ahead with MRP.
- Include people on your software selection/implementation team who have the power to effect change in your organization.
- While DP should not be in charge of the evaluation process, it should have a coordinating role and ensure that the selected software is compatible with the existing system.
- Start off with the simplest possible system to get the job done. Embellish later, if at all.
- Do not blindly toss out subsystems that work. On the other hand, don't try and force an inadequate system to perform beyond its capabilities.
- Use an agreed upon standard for MRP II as a reference for documenting your existing system.
- Workable software can be purchased from either hardware or software vendors. It may also be possible to construct a workable system from software that already exists within the company and some new development. But writing an MRP II system from scratch is a guaranteed losing proposition.

Chapter 4

The Evaluation Process

Part 1: Separating Wheat from Chaff

Like sex drives, card tricks and the weather, computers tend to be discussed in terms of results rather than processes, which makes them rather scary.
(Martin Mayer, American writer)

Many companies getting into the software selection process see it as an awesome task. "After all," they think, "with 150 to 200 packages on the market, just cutting the list will mean we have to contact all the vendors, review their literature, and do a high level evaluation. Don't we have to spend several months just coming up with the final list of candidates?"

Fortunately, the answer is "no." A company that sets out to evaluate and select software in three months cannot possibly contact 150 vendors and conduct in-depth evaluations of their MRP II packages— four to six systems would realistically be the maximum. But that doesn't pose a dilemma; four to six packages are more than an adequate pool to choose from and make an informed buying decision. The fact is, nearly every company can cut their list down to half a dozen or less within several weeks of beginning the software search. And while they're reviewing these packages, they can also investigate their existing system at the same time and determine which subsystems can be salvaged or adapted.

This chapter and the two that follow it provide practical ways for cutting down the potential universe of MRP II software to a manageable size, performing an in-depth functional evaluation of the candi-

71

dates, and factoring into the decision a number of important and related functional issues.

Most of the points below are related to software selection for companies that are getting into MRP for the first time, or that are operating an MRP II system at less than maximum levels of performance and want to improve that performance. They are equally valid, however, for companies that are operating MRP II at high Class B or even Class A levels and wish to switch software, and for companies that want to replace technically outmoded subsystems. Regardless of the situation, the following approach will enable a company to establish quickly which packages are worth serious investigation.

CUTTING THE LIST QUICKLY

Think for a moment about the process of buying a car. One method would be to investigate every possible alternative, then visit every showroom in a six-state area and test drive every car on the lot. Another method would be to investigate a small number of acceptable alternatives by defining a set of criteria by which the list can be cut. This list might include car size, price range, type of manufacturer (for example, domestic versus foreign), performance, etc. You would then locate a few sources within a close geographic area and test drive a limited number of products. Obviously, only the second approach makes sense; it would take months, maybe years, to implement the first one.

A prepared car buyer defines criteria that include such categories as budget constraints, "essential" features, recommendations from experts, maintenance, performance, and safety ratings from objective sources. One or more of these will probably pare down the total universe of automobiles.

The same kind of criteria list can be used to whittle down the number of potential MRP software packages that your company will evaluate:

1. Existing computer hardware and software.
2. Computer power required to support the company.
3. The vendor's proven track record.

4. Recommendations from knowledgeable people.
5. The price range of the software.
6. Innovative data base processing techniques.

1. EXISTING HARDWARE AND SOFTWARE.

Companies with a computer and system software are generally in an enviable position when it comes to selecting application software. The type of computer and data base management system they are using today will probably eliminate 80 percent or more of the packages on the list. For example, a company with an IBM 4361, DOS/VSE, and IDMS can immediately cut down the population of applicable software to five or six packages. For popular minicomputers like the DEC VAX, IBM System/38, or Hewlett-Packard HP-3000, a company would need to review fewer than 10 systems.

Keep in mind that technical constraints are typically not a drawback—there are MRP II software packages for virtually every computer on the market. See Appendix E for a reference of lists and directories on MRP/MRP II/DRP software.

2. COMPUTER POWER REQUIRED.

For companies without existing hardware, part of the process of cutting the list of alternatives will probably be based on a hardware analysis. This analysis needs to consider the current state of the business and its anticipated rate of growth, as well as the growth path provided by various hardware alternatives. Because the analysis must match hardware capabilities to anticipated growth, it may be necessary to bring in specialized assistance in reviewing the situation and making the proper decision.

The process of analyzing hardware requirements for a given company is beyond the scope of this book. However, it is possible to say that careful research in a company may determine a number of constraints like the need for a computer that will support a certain number of terminal devices, will support a business of a particular size (dollars, number of employees, number of item numbers and bills of material, etc.), and transaction volume (35,000 on-line transactions per day), will allow business growth of X percent per year for Y years without conversion, or that is acceptable to the corporate management

information services (MIS) department. Such constraints may eliminate certain hardware and software candidates. For example, knowing
that you will eventually have 30 to 50 workstations would probably
eliminate software running on networked IBM PC's. In some cases, it
would mandate a certain class of computer, such as a midrange minicomputer about the size of the IBM System 38, DEC VAX, or NCR
Tower, or an entry level mainframe like an IBM 4361 computer. Finally, your company's needs might require a specific type of operating
system, perhaps UNIX and its derivatives.

As you can see, defining a range of computing power is one way,
although not necessarily the easiest way, to eliminate a number of
candidates. In combination with criteria explained below, it may help
reduce the list to four to six legitimate possibilities.

3. PROVEN TRACK RECORD.

Does the vendor have a proven track record in supporting Class A or
Class B MRP II users? By limiting the list of software vendors to those
with clients operating at Class A or Class B levels of performance, you
can reduce your risk as you implement MRP II and also reduce the
number of evaluations that have to be conducted.

Granted, by taking this recommendation you will probably eliminate
most, if not all, ''state-of-the-art'' software packages. But as we have
seen so often before, the risk involved in implementing an unproven
piece of MRP II software is unacceptable. Remember Dave Garwood's
rule of thumb: when buying an unproven package, add a year of delay
and double the out-of-pocket cost of the software.

4. PRICE RANGE OF THE SOFTWARE.

MRP II software ranges from $50,000 to $150,000 for minicomputers,
and can go as high as $1,000,000 for mainframe software. Although a
sixty million dollar company can probably pay off a million dollar
software package in about 10 months, there are some significant cash
flow implications of buying this type of software—even more so if you
have to purchase hardware as well. For example, a company purchasing a million dollar MRP II software package will have cash requirements of $1,000,000 in the first year of the implementation while the
benefits from MRP II will come later and over a period of time.

Any company purchasing software should understand the cash requirements of various software decisions, and *if necessary* reduce the potential packages based on price. However, a company should also recognize that implementing MRP II successfully will probably pay back the cost of nearly any software package, so that an arbitrary cutting of the list based on price may not be the most sensible decision. And eliminating the software that best fits your existing technical environment as a way to reduce software prices may end up costing more in the end.

Companies who have to cut the list of potential vendors based on the initial cash required to purchase the software, and can do so because they are not locked into an existing technical environment, can take some comfort from the following: there is little connection between price and functionality. Some of the most functional software available today sells for less than $200,000—and there are several packages in the under-$50,000 range that are as functional as the Cadillacs of mainframe MRP II software.

Just remember, the payback from MRP II is what's important, not how much or how little you spent on software.

5. INNOVATIVE DATA PROCESSING TECHNOLOGY.
During the next few years the field of data processing will change dramatically. New technology, tools, and approaches (like relational data base management systems, fourth generation languages, computer aided systems engineering, and prototyping) promise to reduce the effort required to develop and modify systems. In some cases, the development of systems can be pushed down to the users by providing flexible report writing and systems development tools. Examples of vendors who provide fourth generation tools today include Xerox (IBM mainframe computers), Mitrol (IBM mainframes), and QAD Systems (UNIX and XENIX based micros and minis). Some companies may wish to implement new systems using this newer technology, and if so, this would be a legitimate means of cutting the list.

6. RECOMMENDATIONS FROM KNOWLEDGEABLE PEOPLE.
Anyone getting into MRP II should be using an outside source to help them implement the system as quickly as possible. Most consultants and experts who have been working in the field for some time and who have Class A credentials have probably worked with a number of dif-

ferent software packages directly, or have indirect knowledge of the packages available by virtue of being in the industry. Such an individual with a broader base of experience should be able to suggest several packages that are worth looking at.

To avoid ownership and accountability problems later, it's important that an outsider does not recommend a specific system. Rather, the idea is for the consultant to help reduce the list. You might ask, then, "How can a consultant cut the list for us without doing a detailed evaluation of all our needs?" In most cases, you won't just bring in a consultant at the list-cutting stage; he will have been on board much earlier in the process of preparing for MRP, and will therefore have a handle on major issues in running your business. Besides, given a set of basic criteria (for example, the software must be reasonably functional, operate on a given piece of hardware or operating system, or support a business of a particular size and growth rate), any good outside counsel can help reduce the list rapidly.

Some people may object to the arbitrariness of list cutting, noting that there may be an excellent software package for your company, but that in the process of reducing the list quickly, that package may be dropped from the running. The answer? There's no guarantee that won't happen. But it's an acceptable risk. Remember, the stakes are too high today to operate without MRP II, and less-than-perfect software can be used to get the benefits of MRP. If you still have qualms about it, reread Chapter 1 and then get on with the job.

It is safe to say that one or more of the criteria can almost certainly be used to cut the list quickly and effectively. For example, many companies will find that the first criteria (existing hardware and software) eliminates most contenders; many larger companies will already have a computer, and of them, few will be likely (or would be well advised) to toss out their hardware for the sake of running a particular software package. Other companies will find that knowing the amount of computing power required along with recommendations from knowledgeable people will reduce the list to a few software suppliers.

Remember, in the end you'll be judged on whether you were a responsible consumer of MRP II software, whether you made an informed choice for your company, and whether you got the job done in a reasonable period of time. Any logical method or combination of methods that reduces the list to a valid subset of the population should be used.

Once you've pared down the list of vendors, you're ready to evaluate each candidate's software in terms of functionality. Chapter 5 describes various approaches to performing a functional evaluation of MRP II software, and explains how to get the job done in the shortest amount of time. Chapter 6 shows you how to complete the evaluation by considering technical issues that are not necessarily related to software functionality, but are nevertheless vitally important to making the right software choice.

SUMMARY

- Your goal should be to conduct in-depth evaluations on no more than four to six MRP II software packages within a three month period.
- To reduce the universe of possible contenders, identify basic technical or performance criteria; in most cases, especially when hardware is a constraining factor, the list will shrink to a manageable number.
- Don't fear losing the "best" package in the process of creating a vendor short-list. In the world of MRP II there is no best software package.

Chapter 5
The Evaluation Process
Part 2: Does It Work?

If you think of "standardization" as the best that you know today, but which is to be improved tomorrow—you get somewhere.
(Henry Ford, automobile manufacturer)

Companies performing functional evaluations of MRP II software packages often spend most of their time in a point-scoring exercise that focuses primarily on which package has which features, options, switches, capabilities, etc., and how well they score. Such an exercise avoids the real issue of identifying what must be done to the software to make it work as an MRP II system. Worse, it spends an enormous amount of money and the time and effort of a company's best people.

THE CHECKLIST APPROACH

The most common (and seemingly the easiest) way to evaluate the functionality of an MRP II package is to develop a checklist of desired features and compare each package against it. The checklist can be prepared using:

1. The literature in the field.
2. What people in your company believe is important.
3. The specifications for your existing systems.
4. A listing of the different features of the software package that you've already decided to buy.

79

5. A commercially available checklist from one or more of the large
   consulting firms.
6. A checklist provided by one of the software companies.
7. Any or all of the above.

After compiling a checklist, there are several methods for making the actual product comparisons. One is to research each package in detail. This, however, is usually the least popular method among people who use the checklist approach. More commonly, the checklist is mailed to each of the candidate vendors with a cover letter. The cover letter requests that the vendor answer the questions in the checklist, identifying those functions that are part of the software package and work properly, those functions that are not part of the software package, and those functions that exist partially. In some cases, the vendor will be asked to estimate the effort required to provide a missing feature.

While it is certainly easy to ask the vendors to do your homework, the results are often less than desirable. The best illustration comes from one of my MRP II software evaluation classes, in which there happened to be several software vendors. "I'm not ashamed to admit that I get these RFP's in the mail all the time," said one vendor in defense of the practice. "And each time I get one I do the same thing— I answer 'yes' to all the questions. I figure I have to survive the first cut, and in most cases the company that sent the checklist either doesn't know what features they're asking for, and even if they did, they really don't need them anyway. So I say 'yes' to stay in the evaluation process and then plan on straightening out any problems or misconceptions at the end."

Not all vendors take that approach, however. Another in the class said to me, "I deep six those things when they come in the door. After all, in most cases the checklists are written up based on the specific features of someone else's package—the company is simply trying to justify a selection they've already made. Unless I've already been working with the company and know that we've been selected, I don't waste my time."

Yet a third vendor in the class related his experience with the checklist: "Not long ago I received one in the mail that I felt our company should respond to. There were a number of points that needed clarification, however, and several that didn't make any sense at all in terms of how a company would normally be managed using MRP II. And there were also some questions that didn't make sense because of the type of business the particular company was in. Having worked in the industry for a number of years, I knew that they didn't need certain of the capabilities that they had listed in the checklist. So I called them up and scheduled a visit to their company to review the checklist with the goal of understanding why they had listed certain points. Oddly enough, when I got to the company, they didn't want to talk about the checklist—every time I brought up the subject they wanted to discuss something else. I was pretty determined though, and eventually I got them to talk about the list. What I eventually discovered was that they had contracted with a large consulting firm to perform an analysis of their business and tell them what they needed in software. They hadn't done any education on MRP II, and so they didn't even understand what some of the points on the checklist meant!''

As you can see, although the checklist is commonly used and is superficially appealing, there are some serious drawbacks, including:

1. No one checks the logic of the system to determine whether the feature works normally.
2. A listing of items on a checklist is easy to misinterpret.
3. There is usually no easy way to distinguish essential features or functions from bells and whistles.
4. In most cases, the systems that do best against the checklist are the most complicated.
5. It's easy to confuse this process with the process required to justify the software to management.

The first difficulty with the checklist approach is really the most serious, because it means that no one will ever assess the logic of the system and what must done to make the system work properly. Regardless of how long you make the list, there will not be sufficient detail to determine whether any particular function actually works in a normal manner. This is because the mere presence of a function gives no indications about the correctness of its underlying logic.

To appreciate the kind of trouble that can result when the logic isn't checked, consider an incident in which Ace Flow, a pump manufacturer, hired a major accounting firm to analyze a ''state-of-the-art''

MRP II package that it was planning to purchase and implement. The consultants spent weeks of time analyzing the package, and did a fine job of comparing it to a checklist that consisted largely of data elements and report names. Since it seemed to have everything on their list, they recommended the package to the company, which in turn bought and installed it. Within several months, though, Ace Flow had begun to realize that there were major problems with the system. A detailed review of the system logic revealed the source of the problem: no master scheduling capability and major flaws in the logic of material requirements planning. Although the system documentation listed the proper data elements and had reports with the proper names, no one had checked the basic logic of the system to make sure it worked properly. In other words, the company had bought a package that was seriously flawed and which required major revisions prior to being able to support MRP II!

As the Ace Flow example demonstrates, with the checklist approach it is very possible for the patient to die even though the operation is successful. This brings us to a related flaw with the checklist approach: it does not distinguish essential functions from superfluous bells and whistles. In fact, it encourages users to seek unnecessary functions simply because other people suggest that they be added to the roster.

Another serious flaw in the checklist approach is that it tends to point to the most complicated package as the ''best.'' As I've stressed in the first part of this book, all MRP II software must be modified to one degree or another—there is no perfect software. Too often, the package that scores best on the checklist is the most difficult to modify, and the package that doesn't do quite as well but is simpler and easier to tailor is a better all-around choice. A well-informed buyer looks for an MRP software package that is functionally complete but that does not include unnecessary functions or options. And a well-informed buyer understands the implications of complexity in software.

THE ALTERNATIVE APPROACH: USING A STANDARD SYSTEM

The only effective methods for evaluating MRP II software are those that probe the system's underlying logic, identify specific changes that must be made, and determine whether the changes can be made in the available time. The cornerstone to any method that accomplishes these objectives is having a widely accepted and agreed upon standard for both the functions that need to be part of a system, and the logic that underlies those functions. For example, for MRP II software, the Oliver Wight Companies publish a research report, *The MRP II Standard System* (sometimes called *The Standard System*), that is generally accepted as the definition of the minimum set of functionality needed in an MRP II system. *The Standard System* documents the kernels of logic and the key functions needed for planning and scheduling.

By using an agreed upon standard as the basis for comparison, a company evaluating software can be sure that the essential features—the functions that must be in place to make progress with MRP II—are checked. And by tailoring the standard to its own business, a company can also be sure that it has checked both the essential functions of MRP II as well as the specific (major) functions needed to operate its business. But does that mean you should toss out a contending MRP II package at the point where it deviates from the agreed upon standard? Does it mean that you should expect few if any problems in the fundamental logic of the software packages that you are reviewing (i.e. the package has been around for a while and has lots of users, so it must work properly) and that the problems are more likely in the areas more specific to your business? Or does it mean that you should use the standard as you would use a checklist of functions (i.e. simply verify that the function exists without getting down to the details of its logic)?

The answer is "no" to all of the above. If you eliminate a software package the instant it deviates from your agreed upon standard, you will quickly cut the list of candidates to zero. And our experience with software is that every package has some functional problems, even popular packages that have been available for a decade or more. In fact, our experience shows that there isn't an MRP II software package sold today that has all the functions listed in *The MRP II Standard System*. (See Figure 5.1 for a list of functions missing or in need of modification in a typical MRP II package.)

Assuming that you are going to use the Oliver Wight research document as the basis for your comparison, bear in mind the following:

1. *The Standard System* is a core set of functions that we believe must be present in a software package if it is to be considered a

1. Master production scheduling functions, including:
   Ability to state master production schedule as statement of production
   Physical display of master schedule information
   Available to promise calculation
   Two level master scheduling
   Final assembly scheduling

2. Purchasing functions, including:
   Vendor scheduling   .
   Vendor negotiation support
   Scheduling of incoming inspection
   Outside processing support

3. Input output control

4. Distribution resource planning

5. Tool planning and scheduling

6. Financial planning interfaces, including:
   Projected inventory valuations
   Cash flow projections

Figure 5.1
Commonly missing major capabilities

generalized MRP II system. While some functions are universally necessary, such as the netting logic that makes rescheduling assumptions, others may not be necessary to run your type of business.

For example, if you do not have a product that has many options, you will probably not need logic for two level master scheduling (Topic 2, Point 5) or final assembly scheduling (Topic 5, Point 3). Without distribution centers, branch warehouses, or interplant shipments, you probably shouldn't worry about software that includes a distribution resource planning system (Topic 10); a tooling subsystem (Topic 11) will only be required if you have large numbers of tools that have to be planned and scheduled; and disassembly, sorting, and byproducts (Topic 3, Point 6) is only of use if you have products that are brought back for refurbishment and the parts returned to stock, or a process with byproducts.

To sum up, the points that are not appropriate for your type of business or your industry should be tailored out. As a wise man once said, "If you don't have the problem, don't look for the solution."

2. The flip side of the above point is that some functions are specific to certain industries, and are not included in *The Standard System*. The reason is that the document does not attempt to describe every conceivable function that could be part of an MRP II system. Instead, it tries to identify the broad category of functions that must be part of a system in order to operate MRP II. The primary emphasis is the fundamental logic of the system, not special or peripheral logic that may exist or need to be part of a system for one specialized business or industry.

Nevertheless, certain features not listed in *The Standard System* may be essential to running certain types of businesses, and they need to be included in the packages being reviewed or else easily added to the systems. For example, companies in the pharmaceutical business require lot traceability logic to satisfy the Food and Drug Administration. Many of these same companies need to be able to store inventory quantities to decimal precision. Likewise, companies that are prime defense contractors or, in some cases, first or second tier subcontractors to a prime contractor typically require CSCSC (cost schedule control system criteria, or CSPEC) reporting capabilities.

In these cases, the users (or the users with assistance from their MRP II consultant) will have to determine which functions are essential to making MRP II work in the company. If special functions are going to be added, they should be deferred until after the initial education—otherwise there will likely be a number of non-essential points added to system. Equally important, the logic underlying any additional features must be defined specifically and without ambiguity.

3. Some general features are not included in *The Standard System*, yet are essential to running a business. For example, order entry is a vital function in any company. General ledger, accounts payable, and accounts receivable are similar vital functions. These systems are discussed only briefly, if at all, because

the document was designed to represent a basic set of functionality for planning and scheduling. Part of the decision on what to include was based on the fact that most larger companies already have an operating order entry system and working financial reporting systems, and probably won't change them if they switch MRP II software or acquire one for the first time.

As in the case of adding any new features to the configuration presented in *The Standard System*, you must carefully define the logic and do it in such a way that a vendor can respond.

Before reading about how you can use a source like *The Standard System* as the basis for evaluating an MRP II software package, take a moment to think about what you're trying to achieve with your evaluation. As you conduct your evaluation, plan on having to add some functions, rather than finding the single piece of software that has it all. Also, focus on the positive: "How can I make this package work?" and how serious is this problem—can I work around it or is it essential that it be fixed prior to putting MRP II on the air. Finally, whenever possible corroborate your findings with the MRP II consultant who is working with your company. This can greatly reduce the time spent getting through the process.

Putting an Agreed Upon Standard to Work

Figure 5.2 lists some of the different ways that you can use an agreed upon standard in evaluating the functionality of a piece of software. Assuming that you are willing to invest the effort to research systems properly, the most effective method for reviewing software will be based on a functional analysis of the documentation, and includes the following steps:

Step 1.   Read the documentation.
Step 2.   Meet with the software vendor and use the standard as the agenda.
Step 3.   Review sample or test output.
Step 4.   Seek comments of other users.

Recommended method
Documentation review
Vendor meeting using Standard System as the agenda
Review sample or test output
Seek the comments of other users
Tie the results of the comparison with the Standard System to the software contract

Alternate method
Vendor meeting using Standard System as the agenda
Install demonstration version of software on company computer
Test software against Standard System
Seek the comments of other users
Tie the results of the comparison with the Standard System to the software contract

Wrong method
Develop a checklist from Standard System
Ask the vendors to ''rate themselves''
Get caught up in a point-scoring exercise that tries to demonstrate that one package is better than another
Assume that if the functions look OK on paper, they work in practice—so there's no sense contacting other users
Sign the standard contract

Figure 5.2
Methods for using the Standard System to evaluate MRP II software

Step 5.   Tie the results of your comparison with the standard to the contract.

Reviewing the Documentation

The first order of business in a functional analysis of software is to get a *complete* set of the vendor's documentation. This documentation should include both user and technical documentation, particularly those manuals that deal with logic, processing, edits, and other key aspects of the program. The idea of getting a complete set is that it is better to skim all of it, and skip those parts that you don't need, than to have a sample of the documentation that doesn't contain the information required to determine the presence or lack of essential features and their underlying logic.

Many vendors will gladly turn over documentation if you appear to be a serious prospect, while others will require that you sign a non-disclosure agreement. There is nothing wrong with signing a non-disclosure agreement, as long as the language is reasonable. (An example of a non-disclosure agreement that affords both protection to the vendor and flexibility to the potential customer or consultant can be found in Appendix F.).

Once you've worked out any disclosure issues and have acquired a set of documentation, someone needs to understand and analyze it in order to make the initial evaluation of the software package. In many cases, the person assigned to the task will be from the systems or DP departments, since their staff members are used to reading software documentation. The job, however, might just as well be done by an experienced person from the manufacturing department. Some companies even prefer to have an outsider do the documentation review and chair the subsequent vendor meeting, to gain an additional objective opinion. If you do choose to have an outside reader, make sure that the project team actually participates in the vendor meeting and later steps of the review, otherwise you may encounter problems of ownership and accountability.

For the sake of the following explanation, assume that you are the person in charge of reviewing the documentation. Prior to actually reading the documentation verify the following:

1. You have an agreed upon, well-understood, and tailored (if necessary) standard as the basis for comparison.
2. You have a thorough understanding of how the normal logic for each function specified in the standard should work. In addition, you should have a good understanding of different acceptable alternatives within these functions. (You need to be able to identify which features do not precisely operate in the normal manner, but which are workable.)
3. You've prepared some evaluation worksheets by listing the major evaluation points from your tailored version of the agreed upon standard. Normally this would be done by listing all the points from a topic (or a topic and subheading) together on a page. These work-

sheets are used to organize the effort and to serve as ''memory jog-gers'' that remind you to cover all the needed functions of the system.

Most people evaluating software using this method should plan on two readings of the documentation. One of these readings would skim the documentation for a general understanding of the system; the second reading would be an in depth reading for the details behind the various essential functions of the system.

The objectives of the two readings of the documentation are:

1. Reading #1: to gain a general understanding of the software; which major functions seem to be in place, the basic architecture of the system, and any problems that seem to be ''show-stoppers.''
2. Reading #2: to begin to draw specific conclusions about the packaging by identifying the following:
   a. Those functions of the system that do, in fact, correspond to functions in the agreed upon standard, and that have the proper logic.
   b. Those functions that correspond to the standard system but seem to have logic problems.
   c. System options that must be used in a particular way to operate MRP II in a normal manner.
   d. Functions that are part of the software that are inconsistent with operating a Class A MRP II system and that shouldn't be used at all.
   e. Functions that are missing from the system and that have to be added.

In the second reading of the vendor's documentation, start making notes about how the vendor's software actually works. These notes must include a description of the specific logic used in each feature. You may also wish to describe (or draw pictures) of interrelationships between files, describe edit rules on transactions, and list major data elements used in the system. In addition, functions that are part of the system but don't work properly should be identified for discussion with the vendor. Global options in the system (for example, control file options) should also be identified.

Many people find it helpful to make notes on the worksheets and to attach selected pages of documentation, sample transaction formats, and display or report formats from the documentation. Doing so makes it easy to reconstruct how the logic of the system works and why a particular question or concern has arisen. In the end, a company probably winds up with 20 to 30 pages of actual notes and an additional 30 to 50 pages taken from the documentation.

The final result of this reading and note-taking process is a fairly detailed understanding of how the software is designed to operate, the potential complexity of the software, and possible problems that have to be resolved. Where worksheets are blank, there is compelling evidence that major functions are either not part of the system or are going to be difficult to implement because of the lack of documentation. A good rule of thumb is: If there's no documentation, there's no software.

One last subtle point needs to be mentioned regarding vendor documentation: watch for changes in the tense. The word "will" is a sure tip off for "later release." Every time you encounter "will," make a note in your outline. You'll want to bring it up during your meeting with the vendor, which is the next step in the process.

The Vendor Meeting: Testing the Vendor's Mettle

After completing the documentation review, most companies find it useful to share the findings with the members of the selection team. This helps everyone prepare for the vendor meeting and makes each team member aware of the potential problems in the software package. Once your team understands the situation, it should plan on meeting with the vendor. In some companies, the entire team might visit the vendor site. In other companies, a subgroup might meet with the vendor at a local office. In still other companies, it may be the team or the subteam meeting with the vendor at their own site. The specific location of the meeting, and the number of people from your company, are less important than who attends from the software vendor.

Plan on using your standard as the agenda for the vendor meeting. The notes and documentation that you've assembled from your documentation review will assist in directing the conversation to those areas that are potential problems; in effect, they will help you quickly verify those areas that work properly and zero in on the needed changes or missing functions.

Some portion of the day should be reserved for a demonstration of the system, although this is of secondary importance. My experience with software is that many packages show well, but work poorly. A canned demonstration easily avoids problems and provides little insight into the logical workings of the system. If you are going to see a demonstration, it should verify, at a high level, that the software actually exists. It should also reveal the on-line functionality and human engineering of the system, and produce a level of comfort on the software.

An important aspect of the vendor meeting and/or demonstration is the level of technical expertise of the representatives from the vendor's company. Given the nature of the questions that will probably arise, and the need to deal with specific logic in the system, the software vendor should be prepared to bring a knowledgeable person from the technical or support staff to the meeting. In some instances, a salesman will be able to handle these kinds of questions. Even in those cases it is generally better to spend the time with the technical people, as the following incident reveals.

Several years ago my friend and associate, John Dougherty, and I performed a software evaluation on a package with limited documentation. Prior to having the vendor meeting, we invited our client company to attend and participate in the meeting. "No," said the client company. "We feel comfortable with the system and just want to have an independent assessment to verify our conclusions. We don't see any real point in spending a day meeting with the vendor's technical people."

When we met with the vendor (who incidentally brought in *all* of the people who would be responsible for supporting the package), we were shocked to discover that the technical staff had no idea of how the logic of the system they were supporting actually worked. Our initial comments in the meeting were to ask about the incompleteness of the documentation on the basic logic of material requirements planning, and to ask the group to walk us through it. One of the technical people responded with a basic definition of what netting logic is all about, delivered in less than 45 seconds. We then repeated our request for a detailed explanation of the logic, only to be treated to an hour of circular explanations that at several points conflicted with what documentation there was on the system. Even more telling, if the explanations that the vendor's technical staff gave were correct, the package would have been incapable of doing MRP. Finally, we suggested looking at the actual programs for MRP, which they grudgingly divulged and which we traced line by line. In the end, we wound up explaining to the vendor how his own netting logic worked.

Aside from the lack of confidence that the meeting inspired, it indicated several serious problems that our client would likely encounter down line if he bought the package. First, the software did not work normally and along the lines of a standard system, and the client company was not aware of the problems. A more serious problem was that the vendor was incapable of supporting the package from a technical perspective even in those areas that worked properly! If there was ever a reason for meeting with the vendor's support and technical staff, this is it.

Of course, this is not to say that all vendors are ignorant of their own systems. Many have a very thorough understanding of how their product works and how it stacks up to an agreed upon standard. And if you do not have people on your staff who are capable of doing a review, you might have no choice but to turn to the vendor for bottom-line answers. However you obtain the results, though, the vendor meeting is the time to identify deficiencies and discuss how the functional areas they represent may be shored up, improved, or expanded. And those decisions, of course, must all be cast in a contract (see Chapter 7).

In many ways, the meeting with the vendor is the acid test of whether his software has what your company needs, and whether he will be able to support it. It will also be an opportunity to identify features and functions that are implied to be forthcoming, but which a salesman is unwilling to identify publicly. Remember those ''wills'' you jotted down during your second reading of the documentation? Now is the time to convert them into ''whens'' by asking the vendor to provide hard dates for each feature or function that is not presently in existence or not presently operational.

Finally, in regard to functions that you identified as not working normally and along the lines of the explanation in a standard system, there should be a discussion of the size of the effort to fix the problem, who has to make the change, and what the effect will be on the soft-

ware warranty. If you walk away from this meeting without understanding the major changes for which you will be responsible and without concurrence on the time schedule for the vendor-supplied
modifications, you will have failed in your responsibilities.

Shortcuts and Pitfalls

At this point you might ask, "Is all this laborious work really necessary? Why not just go to the vendor and say, 'We're using *The MRP
II Standard System* as the basis for our evaluation—we'd like to have
a meeting with you to discuss how your software covers each of the
points it describes.' " You could take this approach, and some companies do. But with MRP, as with many things in life, any shortcut
has its shortcomings. This shortcut is the checklist approach explained
earlier in this chapter. And as we've seen, anytime you skip the logic
checking portion of the software evaluation, you will be surprised later.

Reviewing Sample Output

For software evaluations based on a documentation review, an important step following the vendor meeting is reviewing sample or test
output. The point here is that you shouldn't try to test every function
of the software package, but rather should try to verify some of the
basic numbers, and to understand which reports various individuals
will be using (for example, how many reports display the following
information to a planner: basic descriptive information, the time phased
display, pegging, supporting details to scheduled receipts and firm
planned orders, and exception messages). In my experience, software
packages with major problems often exhibit those problems in a very
small amount of sample or test output.

User Reaction

In the final phase of evaluating the functionality of the software, a
responsible buyer should contact some users of the system as a way to
gain some assurance that the software works without problems. Most
well-informed software purchasers make it a point to visit at least one
user of the software package and to talk by phone with several more

references. Generally, the software vendor should be expected to provide the names of the companies for the user reference.

The method used to choose user references is also important. Ideal references are companies operating MRP II at Class A or Class B levels of performance, because these companies will be exercising most of the system's functions in a normal way. Companies that are operating the system at Class C (or poorer) levels of performance can still be valuable as references, but it should be understood that they may not be using the functions of the system as they should be used. In other words, there may be problems in the software that are not apparent to them. Alternately, they may believe there are problems or deficiencies in the system when, in fact, there are not.

The least valuable user reactions are likely to come from companies that have only recently purchased the software and are not operating much, if any, of their business using the new tools provided in the system. Unfortunately, many MRP II software packages (some of it good and some of it bad) have been sold over the years through the "Bandwagon Approach," in which a whole series of companies jump on board and purchase what appears to be a popular package without checking the status of those who have gone before.

Some suggested questions from Oliver Wight's *The Standard System* provide guidance in interviewing companies using a particular software package:

Stage of Implementation. What software modules are being used, and for how long? The objective is to determine whether the functions in the software have been exercised.

Functionality. Do the functions explained in the system documentation and by the vendor work? The objective is to determine whether or not the system documentation and the vendor accurately understand and have accurately explained the functions in the system.

Bugs. Did the users of the system experience significant bugs in working with the system? Notice that the word "significant" is used here. Experience seems to indicate that all systems have bugs. A small bug that does not disrupt operations, however, is a different matter from one that halts progress and slows down the implementation.

Vendor Support. How do the users of the system rate the support provided by the vendor?

Users. Do the people using the system like it? What features or changes would make them feel better about it?

Other. Are there any comments about the system that would be of interest to people considering the system, such as the documentation, maintenance, run time, and other important aspects?

Doing a Documentation Review of an Existing "Home-Grown" System

For people who have an existing piece of software that was developed over a period of years and which is being evaluated as an MRP II software alternative, the above methods present some apparent difficulties. First there is the relative lack of documentation to use as the basis of a review. *Any* system will have some documentation, however, and it can be examined according to the steps just described. As for the vendor meeting and user queries, you can call a joint meeting of the systems and data processing people who wrote and support the system and the users from various departments who have been operating the system. As in the case of the meeting with a software vendor, the basic intent of the meeting is to thrash out an understanding of the program, identify the major problems, and plan how the limitations can be eliminated.

A consultant can be helpful in this process, because of his objectivity and impartiality. Since he has no vested interest in the software, he can mediate any problems between the two groups. It's essential that the people who developed the system *and* the people who use it sit in the same room and come to a consensus on the logic of the system. More often than not, each group knows something about the system that the other does not. So however you achieve it, achieving common knowledge is the first step to making intelligent decisions about this alternative.

ALTERNATIVE TO USING DOCUMENTATION AS THE BASIS FOR A REVIEW

While the preceding method for evaluating MRP II functionality was based on a thorough review of the documentation, another workable method entails actually testing the functions of the system:

Step 1:   Meet with software vendor and use an agreed upon standard as the agenda.

Step 2:   Install a demonstration version of software on an in-house computer or on a time-sharing facility.

Step 3:   Test the functions of software against your custom-tailored standard system. Review the output.

Step 4.   Seek the comments of other users.

Step 5.   Tie the results of your comparison with the standard into a contract.

This method could be the one a company would choose to use if the software existed, but there was little if any documentation. In practice, though, this method doesn't work very well for software available for larger mainframe computers. In general, the software is so complicated that it is virtually impossible to use the software without having read the documentation and attended several software vendor classes.

SUMMARY

- Beware the checklist approach; it does not give you any indication of whether the logic underlying the features of the software package are correct.

- Don't ask a vendor to do your work for you; you'll have to live with the system, and you should use your judgment about what works correctly and what works incorrectly.

- Use an agreed upon standard as a basis for comparison. It contains the basic logic proven necessary to plan and schedule effectively.

- Delete those features from the standard that may not apply to your manufacturing environment, and add those features that are specific to your business. The result will be a custom-tailored standard system suitable for serving as the basis for MRP II software evaluations and contract negotiations.

- Conduct two readings on a *complete* set of the vendor's documentation. Get a general understanding during the first read, and make specific queries on the second. Use your notes as the basis for a meeting with the vendor.
- Seek user reviews of the package you are considering. Select sites that have proven experience with MRP.

Chapter 6

The Evaluation Process
Part 3: Sidelights

It is only when things go wrong that machines remind you how powerful they are.
(Clive James, critic)

A review of the functionality of a software package lies at the heart of any evaluation. But the evaluation would be hardly complete without exploring a number of technical issues that may render an otherwise functionally adequate package useless for your company:

1. Can the required modifications be done within an acceptable time frame?
2. Is the package based on a sound design philosophy, one that encourages people to use their ingenuity rather than blindly relying on the system?
3. Is it really worth the money when compared to other alternatives? What is the *real* cost in terms of delays?
4. Are the run and response time estimates available? How were they developed?
5. Can the package be easily interfaced with modules from other sources, or are you locked into the vendor's entire product line?
6. Is the vendor financially sound?
7. What level of support will the vendor promise?
8. Is the documentation adequate? Can it be accessed and understood by non-technical users?

These considerations are vitally important to your assessment. In the following discussion, we'll see how each one bears on your purchasing decision.

DETERMINING MODIFICATION EFFORTS

By now it's no surprise that an important aspect of investigating any MRP II software package is to identify the modifications that are absolutely essential in order for your company to use the software effectively. Identifying these modifications and assessing the effort required to make them is a byproduct of using an agreed upon standard to review the program's functionality. As you compare the prospective software package against standard, you will find a number of points that are either missing from the package, or that are present but do not work properly. (See Figure 6.1 for a listing of the most common deficiencies in commercial MRP II software packages.) For each point that turns up, you will certainly need to have a discussion with the software supplier and your own systems and data processing group (and perhaps the users as well) regarding how the problem will be fixed.

The goal is to develop a set of high level specifications that can later be used as a blueprint for making changes. The specifications should

---

1. Two level master production scheduling logic.
2. Support for final assembly scheduling.
3. Vendor scheduling.
4. Input output control.
5. Forecasting.
6. Correct logic for handling phantoms, transients, self-consumed assemblies.
7. Problems in the physical display of MRP information.
8. Dispatching of incoming inspection.
9. Tool planning and scheduling.
10. Financial planning interfaces.

Figure 6.1
Most common deficiencies in MRP II software packages

include an estimate of the magnitude of the changes needed to be made, and a mention of who will make them. Figure 6.2 describes typical modification efforts commonly required for off-the-shelf MRP II packages.

Another set of modifications concerns planning for major interfaces. To plan for the interfaces, the vendor must first provide you with a basic understanding of the architecture of the system. Once a certain comfort level has been established, your systems and data processing people can begin plans for both temporary and permanent interfaces.

After you have determined who is responsible for modifications and interfaces, the next step is to develop a plan for actually getting the work done. In making this plan, most companies assume that the vendor will be responsible for most if not all functional modifications, while they will do the temporary and permanent interfaces to existing systems. And unfortunately, companies all too often accept the vendor's schedule for delivering the changes without questioning the consequences of slips in the schedule.

The plan for getting the modifications accomplished has two parts. First, a check for reasonableness: has the vendor or have you ever

1. Two level master scheduling deficiencies—medium sized systems and programming effort.
2. Final assembly scheduling—medium sized effort.
3. Vendor scheduling—small sized effort.
4. Input output control—small to medium sized effort.
5. Forecasting—medium sized effort.
6. Correct logic for handling phantoms, transients, self-consumed assemblies—small to medium sized effort.
7. Problems in the physical display of MRP information—small to medium sized effort.
8. Dispatching of incoming inspection—small sized effort.
9. Tool planning and scheduling—medium to large sized effort.
10. Financial planning interfaces—small to medium sized effort.

Figure 6.2
Typical amount of effort required to fix common functional problems

undertaken a project of this size before? If so, were you able to accomplish the changes within the available time? If you've never undertaken a project of this size, has anyone? What have other companies found necessary to pull off this kind of project successfully?

The second part of the plan for modifications is having a fall-back position, sometimes called "Plan B." In a situation where the software vendor will be making the required changes, it's essential to devise a backup plan, just in case the vendor fails to make the software available in time for implementation. Developing this kind of backup plan also sheds some interesting new light, and a different perspective, on the vendor's plan. Let's suppose you've found a package that lacks capacity planning, but in all other respects is complete. An estimate reveals that developing a simple capacity planning system using in-house programming resources will take one person working full time four months (which, by the way, is probably generous based on my experience). This means that to have a capacity planning system available in month 12, work must start in month eight.

The key question is whether the vendor's delivery date is earlier than your need date. And as you can probably tell from the example, the need date is *not* the date when you plan to start implementing, it's the date you'd have to start programming if the vendor fails to deliver. In our capacity planning system example, the real need date is month eight: if the vendor fails to deliver by that date, programming must start immediately.

At this point, the whole issue of vendor delivery reliability becomes a significant issue. Sadly, delivery reliability for new application software is no better than the delivery reliability of new products of any type. Think about the new products that your own company has introduced over the last five years: how many of them came out on time and working as specified? If your company is like most, your delivery performance to the original promise date for the new product is probably less than 50 percent. And this, regrettably, is probably what you can expect from an average software company with respect to major software improvements. Although there are software vendors with excellent track records with respect to delivering new products on time, the majority are probably going to have unanticipated problems with the improvements that will cause one of two problems:

a. The vendor reviews the problem and decides to make the changes necessary to make the software perform as promised. In most cases, this means significant revamping and a slipped delivery.

b. The vendor reviews the problem and decides to bring the product out with known deficiencies. In this case, the system comes out on time, but may not be usable in the form delivered.

In cases where you truly need some capability promised for a future version of the software, you'll need to assess whether having this particular piece of software and dealing with this particular vendor is worth risking a delay in the implementation: what kind of problems are you going to have if the vendor is late?

In the end, you have to make a decision based on the facts that you gather and an assessement of the risks involved. Review the vendor's plan for developing missing functions, and ask for an explanation of the specific milestones that have to be hit to get the job done. If there is no detailed plan, there is no chance that you'll get the software on time, if at all. If there is a plan, ask for some references so you can get some assurances that the vendor has undertaken a project of this size before and delivered the changes on time. In any case where the fixes or improvements are such that only the vendor can do the work, then you might consider cutting the evaluation of his package, since you may be taking a major risk and jeopardizing the whole project.

ASSESSING DESIGN PHILOSOPHIES

The design philosophy of the vendor has a major impact on the usability of the software. Nothing sums up the matter better than *The Standard System*, which offers these conclusions:

> There are a number of features that are a part of a good software package, but which are not specific functions. These are the design philosophies that have been embodied in the software. A designer who does not understand these philosophies will produce a package with limitations or fundamental flaws. Evidence that a software package does not recognize these design philosophies should be taken as a warning that the software may have hidden flaws or limitations. The most important of these philosophies are the following:

Simulation of Reality. An MRP II system has only one purpose: to accurately simulate the realities of a manufacturing environment. A software package that does not attempt to accurately simulate reality will lose the primary objective of the system.

Simplicity. All truly great things are simple, and MRP II systems are no exception. A software package needs a full set of functions. Any additional features in the system are both unnecessary and undesirable. They generally make the operation of the system overly complicated, and in doing so, destroy its native and inherent simplicity.

Responsibility. Systems don't make things happen, people do. Most things are accomplished because someone is directly responsible for a task or decision. A software package should be designed to support the responsibility requirements for the day-to-day operation of the system. It should not obscure, impede, or try to assume these responsibilities. The people using the system should have direct operating control over the things for which they will be held accountable.

Doing something because the computer said to do it is a lame and unjustifiable excuse. A good software system should recognize the need to present what is happening to the people using the system. It should always provide the information for someone to explain why he or she has taken some kind of action and why what was done makes sense.

Standardization. Standardization is general applicability. A system that adheres to the standards and conventions will be one that has fewer problems in implementation and operation. Standardization lays the groundwork for effective communications and problem solving. It allows the hard fought lessons of the past to be brought forward to today and into the future.

Non-ingenuity. People have the ingenuity to solve the day-to-day operational problems when given a statement of the problem and a clear cut directive to solve it. A good system will point out the problems without attempting to devise a solution. By the time the logic and parameters are designed into a system for solving the endless numbers of situations and occurrences, the system becomes too complicated and cumbersome. Even the designers are likely to wonder if the system will ever work. Instead, the system should allow the people using it to find a solution and then be able to implement the solution within the existing framework of the system.

ASSESSING THE TRUE COST OF THE PACKAGE

Ten years ago, a vendor with a relatively complete mainframe MRP II software package could command any price, even upwards of $500,000. At that time, the cost of the software seemed more directly related to the functional completeness of the software. The more complete, the higher the cost. Today, however, a number of fairly complete packages are entering the market with price tags under $175,000. Now that the power of minicomputers has increased into the range of mainframe computers and very powerful micros have come on the market, many packages for minis and micros are complete enough to compete with the mainframe systems. Consequently, many companies are legitimately questioning whether software in the high end ($500,000 and up) is worth the money. In the final analysis, each company must make its own decision, by estimating the true costs of each software alternative.

The first step in determining whether a particular package is worth the money, regardless of what size computer it is designed for, is to complete the cost justification for implementing the system. The key number, of course, will be the yearly or monthly recurring benefit once MRP II is fully implemented. That number, of course, will also be the cost of delaying bringing MRP II on air.

The second step is to estimate the number of months of delay that will result from having to modify the system. To do this, you must take each major function that will have to be developed or modified. Who will do it? And what might have to be done in terms of installing temporary and permanent interfaces? Who will do the interfacing work? Your own in-house staff? Outside programmers? The vendor? Whoever does the work, *can they do it in the available time?*

To answer the last question, which is a crucial one, look back in history. Has your company, or the vendor, ever done a modification project of the magnitude that will be required in this instance? If so, how much time was planned? How much time did it actually take?

Unless there is absolutely compelling evidence to the contrary, you must use the average delay you've experienced in the past in projects of this size. The tendency is always to say, "But it will be different this time." Experience shows, however, that it almost never is, and you may make a bad decision unless you face the hard facts about software delays.

Step three is to calculate the out-of-pocket expense to bring the system up to the standard and to interface to the systems which are being retained. Note that the estimate is an estimate of putting all the bells and whistles of one system into the other. The estimate is of the additional money needed to get a working minimum system.

Finally, the true cost of a software alternative is the package price (note this may include the cost of the hardware if you are changing) plus out-of-pocket expense, plus the cost of delay (monthly cost of delay times estimated project delay). By using this method, you may discover that what appears to be a relatively inexpensive package might, when the dust settles, wind up costing more than a higher priced package if it requires extensive modifications to make it suitable for your company. For this reason, the "base price + modification price + cost of delay" formula is critical to your evaluation.

CHECKING FOR TECHNICAL REQUIREMENTS

There are generally two types of technical requirements of MRP II software: fixed and flexible. Fixed requirements refer to compatibility with hardware and software already in place, such as the brand of computer, the operating system, or the data base management system. As mentioned earlier in the chapter, if a company has an NCR Tower running UNIX, it will probably need to buy software if it wants to keep using that machine. If it does choose to keep the machine, software compatibility would become a fixed requirement, and could be used to quickly cut the list of possible contenders.

In contrast, flexible technical requirements are more a matter of preference, and include items such as the programming language. For instance, you might prefer COBOL, but you'll accept a program written in PL/I. Likewise, you might be seeking a program written in RPG III for your System 38, but you'll settle for COBOL. In most cases people will have a preference for one, but if the package were otherwise equal, and one had the desired language, that could be the deciding factor.

From a user's standpoint, there are also fixed and flexible requirements. For example, a fixed requirement might be that the software support an on-hand quantity field with three digits of precision. If a software package only supports an integer quantity field for the on-hand balance, the proper approach to implementing the new system is not to round all numbers up (or down) to get integer values. The only situation where you would probably continue to look at a package that didn't support key data field sizes would be when the software package makes it easy (better yet, trivial) to make the change. And today, only a few highly innovative packages have such capabilities. Some examples would be:

1. Software packages that take full advantage of the IBM System/38 architecture
2. Hewlett-Packard's Materials Management/3000 and Production Management/3000
3. Computers running under the PICK operating system
4. Fourth generation language-based systems, such as MITROL (for IBM), and QAD systems (for UNIX machines)

RUN TIME AND RESPONSE TIME

In the old days when systems were more batch oriented, it was less important to do comprehensive or precise run time estimates. As we move more toward online systems, it is increasingly important to have better response times. In other words: it makes little sense to have highly paid people sitting unproductively waiting for the computer to respond. The state-of-the-art is such, though, that it is very difficult to get a precise handle on run and response times. And if you don't have some idea of how long the system will require to process your information, you're likely to be in for an unpleasant surprise.

This means you will have to get an assurance from the vendor, who will have several options at his disposal for assessing response time. One assessment technique the vendor might use is the performance simulator, such as the one provided by Unisys Corporation for its Unis

1100 software. This simulator is a mathematical algorithm which develops a set of volume estimates based on some key factors like the number terminals attached to the system, the number of transactions of each different type, the specific model of computer that the system will run on, the amount of load from other systems, the number of items, bills of material, orders, and other important parameters.

Are such simulations accurate? On the negative side, it is easy enough for the system performance to change (for example, because of a modification) without the mathematical model changing. Such is the risk a vendor runs with the approach. On the positive side, testimony from those who have used the Sperry simulator have reported that for Sperry software, it is remarkably accurate.

Another alternative for the vendor is to set up a benchmark test, in which a data base of a particular size is created and run on the system. This technique is being done at IBM, which developed the original performance estimates for MAPICS by attaching two System 34s to each other. While one machine emulated a terminal network feeding in transactions, the other machine ran the actual system. The machine that emulated the terminal network also had the software that captured the performance statistics. This is a somewhat more accurate performance measurement method than writing a mathematical simulation, because it's based on system reality.

Another innovative approach is used by Formation Inc., a company that developed a performance monitor software program that actually emulates terminals feeding in transactions. With this package, the vendor can set up a data base of a particular size (number of items, number of bills, etc), and then set the emulation software so that it feeds in transactions emulating 25, 60 terminals or whatever the desired number and measures the response time. This generates performance statistics off a live system.

Despite these advances, most vendors will give you performance estimates based on test cases in which he develops profiles that enable him to specify run times for various sized companies. The other common method is for the vendor to provide statistics from a list of users with similar sized data bases. (This also brings us back to an earlier point about only considering software that has a sufficient number of

1. How will you or did you generate performance statistics?
   Customer testing?
   Vendor testing?
   On a dedicated or non-dedicated system. If not dedicated, what was the additional load on the machine?
2. What was the size of the data base against which these statistics were generated?
3. What was the transaction mix used in testing?
4. What was the size of the computer, memory, number of disk drives, etc.?
5. What is the anticipated average response time? By transaction?
6. What is the expected run time for:
   Running the master schedule report?
   Material requirements planning?
   Capacity requirements planning?
   Generating the daily dispatch list?
   Producing the vendor schedule?

Figure 6.3
Common questions to ask about performance estimates

users that you can turn to for their experience. A new package will simply not have the user base to compile performance and other vital statistics.)

If you are getting performance estimates from a vendor, there are a number of questions that need to be asked. (See Figure 6.3 for a detailed list.) In general, though, you will want to know estimates for the average response time, and for major batch jobs. Part of having an understanding as to whether these are acceptable is knowing how frequently these batch jobs will be done. For example, a nine hour run time might be unacceptable if you plan to run MRP each night, but would probably be more than adequate if you plan to run weekly.

Finally, although he may not have the answer, you should ask the vendor to give you information by type of transaction, as well as average response time and run times on anything that is executed fairly frequently, such as MRP, the master production schedule reporting, capacity requirements planning, input output control reporting, the vendor schedule reports, and the daily dispatch list.

EXPLORING OTHER INTERFACING APPLICATIONS OFFERED BY THE VENDOR

Some vendors have interfacing applications that are part of a larger business systems architecture. You may want to use these other applications now or in the future, so their availability may be important. Also, the software design may prevent you from running anyone else's modules. The key point is that some packages can create interfacing problems between other systems, or can force you to write your interfaces.

DETERMINING VENDOR FINANCIAL STRENGTH

It is important to get reasonable assurance that the vendor will be in business from the installation to the time you become self-sufficient. This time span could be as long as five years.

Obviously, you do not want to hand over a check for a hundred thousand dollars or more to someone who might be out of business tomorrow. So you need to know as much about the vendor's financial status and history as possible. Your inquiry into this area should start off as it would when investigating the financial strength of any supplier: get the vendor's financial statements or request a Dun & Bradstreet report. Then analyze the company for past and present performance.

One aspect of investigating a software company is unique and warrants special attention: how are the vendor's development costs being handled on his financial statement? For years, there were two methods for handling development costs. Vendors could treat software as an asset of the corporation and write it off over a period of years, or they could expense development in the year that it occurred.

Capitalizing development costs may cause a software company to look healthier than it may actually be in the years during and just following the development. In the recent past there were several situations where software companies involved in significant amounts of development announced multi-million-dollar profits based on capitalizing costs of development. Had these same companies expensed the costs of development, their financial statements would have shown multi-million-dollar losses. That these companies occasionally run into financial problems isn't all that surprising—what is surprising is that few of the vendors' customers saw it coming. It *was* possible to identify upcoming financial problems, had the customers and prospective customers only done the proper kind of financial analysis or had they even asked people knowledgeable about the software business.

Regrettably, the situation is more confused today. The Securities and Exchange Commission recently ruled that *all* vendors must capitalize some of the cost of development. The specific percentage, though, is left to the choice of the individual vendors. To a non-specialist, this makes the situation worse, not better. Consequently, in the area of analyzing a vendor's financial health you have some limited alternatives:

1. Hire a professional auditor (like someone from one of the Big Eight) to do a detailed analysis.
2. Use available sources (D&B listings, financial statements from the vendor, advice or comments from people who are knowledgeable in the field) and ask the vendor to explain what percentages are used for assigning development costs as assets, and use your judgment in determining whether the software that is carried as an asset really is an asset. (A vendor can easily spend an enormous amount of money developing what turns out to be a poor product that no one wants. In that case, having a worthless product carried as an asset does little to substantiate the vendor's financial strength.)
3. Develop your own method. A venture capitalist once gave me a somewhat tongue-in-cheek guide to determining companies that are about to have problems: "Watch out for the ones that just built a palatial new corporate headquarters or that just bought a new corporate jet." Of course, what he was really saying was that you should be suspicious of extraordinary growth—companies that grow rapidly for a short period of time and quickly adjust their spending to that rapid rate of growth may have significant problems handling a downward turn in business.

However you make the assessment, the results are important for the following reason: when you invest in an MRP II package, you are buying the ability of the vendor to correct problems and support the software at least during your implementation. So you owe it to your company to be sure that whomever you buy from today will be here at least long enough for you to become self-sufficient.

DETERMINING VENDOR SUPPORT

As with any application, vendor support of MRP software is crucial to the usefulness of a particular package. Vendor support includes the following areas: the vendor's people who will be responsible for helping you to implement the system; the ongoing technical support services from the vendor; the training programs available on the system; and the amount of support proposed.

While it is essential that the vendor supply experienced people to help implement the system, it is even more important that your own people ''spill their own blood'' during implementation to lock in their sense of ownership. If a vendor proposes a ''turn-key'' implementation, it's important to find out what he means; if turn-key means ''I'll come in and install hardware and software and then turn the system over to you,'' that's acceptable. If he means ''I'll install the hardware and software and direct the implementation, then turn over a working system to you,'' you're asking for trouble. Such an approach greatly compromises ownership and accountability. Remember: he who implements must ultimately inherit the system.

Another important consideration in the support area is whether a vendor will justify the amount of consulting and training he proposes to give you. While most people would expect a functionally complete, more expensive software package to require less support proposed than a lower priced package, experience suggests the opposite. In fact, based on a survey done in 1981 by Oliver Wight Software Research, in most instances, the support quoted by most vendors was directly proportional to the cost of the software. When the software cost $50,000, the proposed support typically cost less than $20,000. When the software cost $350,000, the proposed support was in the neighborhood of $150,000.

Quantity isn't confused with quality

Logical organization, by function

Effective index exists

Written to reading level of average reader

Technical explanations clear and not redundant

Oriented to getting something done, instead of explaining reports or screens and data elements

Figure 6.4
Characteristics of good documentation

REVIEWING THE QUALITY OF THE VENDOR'S DOCUMENTATION

Documentation is the bane of the software industry, and MRP software vendors are no exception. Given the enormous amount of material that accompanies MRP II software packages—sometimes as much as 40 volumes of information—the quality of the documentation becomes critical. Assuming that the explanations are clear, the most important concern is how well the documentation is organized. Is there an index? Is the index accurate? These questions are very important, because piecing together an explanation from several different sources is not only an exercise in tongue-biting frustration, it is also a poor use of time.

Further, studies cited in the computer press indicate that the quality of the documentation has a major effect on the learning time involved with the new system. Some studies (based on micro software) show that documentation quality can affect learning time by as much as *50 percent*! See Figure 6.4 for a listing of the characteristics of good documentation.

SPECIAL CASE: REVIEWING OBJECT CODE ONLY SOFTWARE

Recently, object code only MRP II software has become popular, and raises some unique problems regarding the missing functionality issue. Object code only software, now offered by several of the large hard-

ware vendors, is neither better nor worse than MRP software distrib-
uted with source code. From a vendor's point of view, however, object
code only software offers two distinct advantages.

First, it protects the vendor's investment in the software. By limiting
the number of people who have access to the source code, a vendor
keeps his trade secrets, special programming techniques, and proprietary software functions from the eyes of competitors. This makes sense,
because even though there is little reason to protect the well-known
general logic of an MRP system, a software vendor with an innovative
approach will have invested a significant amount of time and money in
the effort, and should enjoy whatever level of protection is possible.

Second, object code only software simplifies support, because all
customers will be using a tested version of the system. As a result,
users cannot make changes in the basic system and cause unique problems.

But what is good for the vendor is not necessarily good for the end
user. As we have seen in this chapter, each user will need to make a
number of modifications to the basic software package to accommo-
date his business. In addition to functional modifications and modifications to meet regulatory requirements, users will also want to make
changes in field sizes, report layouts, CRT displays, and transaction
formats. Although these are "cosmetic" changes, they are nevertheless important because they allow a company to tailor the software to
the style and experience of its operators.

When contemplating buying object code only MRP II software, you
must ask key questions such as: What kinds of protection should be
written into the contract? What situations should be avoided? Who is
accountable for making the software work? These and other issues are
discussed in Chapter 7, which covers MRP II software contracts. As a
technical consideration, however, users of object code only software
should look for a package that is as functionally complete as possible,
and allows them to change field sizes, reports, CRT displays, and
transactions. It must also allow them to add additional software to meet
regulatory requirements. If any of these characteristics or capabilities
are missing or cannot be provided in the software, there are likely to
be problems in implementing and operating the system.

At this point, the material covering MRP II software evaluation is complete. In the following chapters we turn our attention to the art of negotiating fair and reasonable contracts, what to do with the software in the early days of the implementation, and how to become self-sufficient.

SUMMARY

- Identifying necessary modifications is a vitally important part of the evaluation process. If modifications cannot be made within an acceptable time frame, forget the package, no matter how good it seems otherwise.

- To be effective, an MRP II package must reflect an appreciation for simplicity, and the knowledge that people will be using the system as a tool for making better decisions.

- Add the cost of making modifications to the purchase cost, and then factor in the cost of delay to determine the *real* cost of a software package.

- Get the vendor to give you a realistic estimate of response and run times.

- Make sure you are aware whether a particular piece of software is compatible with software that must be interfaced.

- Check the vendor's financial strength before you buy. Avoid situations where you'll be forced to support the software yourself before you are ready.

- Beware "turn-key" support systems that promise to install the hardware and software, and then direct the implementation. Your own people have to assume ownership of the system.

- Don't underestimate the value of good documentation—it can dramatically affect how long it takes your company to learn the package. Good documentation is well organized and indexed, and is written for an average non-technical user.

Chapter 7

Let's Make a Deal:

The Fine Art of Negotiating a Software Contract

A verbal contract isn't worth the paper it's written on.
(Samuel Goldwyn, film producer)

Software, like many other things in life, falls into a category of products and services that deserve a well-thought-out contract specifying the obligations of the parties involved. Although there are numerous instances of on-going, trusting relationships between software suppliers and their customers, there are also instances where one of the companies had dramatically different expectations from the other, and where the relationship was neither trusting nor satisfying for either party. A higher than average opportunity for misunderstanding, the (relatively) long term nature of the relationship, and the potential costs of problems if they occur are all reasons why both the software vendor and the client company must work hard to agree upon the contract—and why the contract must adequately protect both parties.

This is especially true in the case of software for two reasons. First, the intangible nature of software and its ease of duplication makes it essential that each company understand what products and services are and are not being provided, where and when they may be used, how the license may be transferred to other parties, and how long the product may be used. Second, because service is as much a part of the decision as the software functions themselves, both companies need to address the support, maintenance, and upgrade issues that are likely to

117

arise, before the relationship begins. In most cases, companies are not purchasing software because of its functionality, but rather because of such factors as vendor reputation, commitment to product improvements, or the underlying technology. These factors should be agreed upon and documented to whatever degree is possible. This is essential to establishing a relationship with ''no surprises,'' and one where both parties understand their mutual responsibilities.

It's easy to lose sight of the fact that a contract protects both sides. From the vendor's point of view, the financial investment in the system is major and deserves to be protected. The product is such that it can be easily copied and redistributed to other locations outside the company or, equally bad, passed out to other unauthorized users within a corporation. In addition, from the perspective of service, the worst users tend to consume the greatest amount of support resources. To the extent that either of these types of problems can be anticipated and avoided, it is to everyone's benefit to do so.

A software contract also protects the licensee. A comprehensive agreement spells out clearly issues such as:

—the specifics of what is being purchased and against what standard the product features can be tested;

—the ownership and license terms;

—what rights each party has to transfer or prevent the transfer of the product to other sites;

—guidelines for support, enhancements, and on-going maintenance;

—who defends whom in case of patent or copyright infringements;

—who owns any custom software developed as part of the software;

—what provisions are made for terminating the agreement between the parties;

—what money must change hands at what times; and

—what penalties are provided for non-conformance or non-delivery.

Methods for dealing with each of these issues have been developed through years of experience and are explained in the rest of this chapter. You will find them applicable to nearly every situation you encounter, with the exception of:

1. Negotiations with IBM. IBM is in the enviable (from a vendor's perspective) position of not changing their standard contract. Except for discounts available to large volume purchasers, IBM has a flat policy: customers sign the standard contract. This reduces the burden of administering the contract and of communicating to a far-flung support staff what the terms of each customer's support are to be.
2. Purchase of software retail. Retail stores are merely go-betweens and cannot typically write a software contract that obligates the vendor to anything. In this case, it's what's inside the shrink wrap that counts.

Assuming that you are dealing directly with the software vendor and that the vendor is not IBM, you can and should negotiate a software contract within several weeks of your decision. The following rules will help you work within that time frame and eliminate common problems.

RULE #1: AVOID AN ADVERSARIAL RELATIONSHIP

Too often, companies purchasing software assume an adversarial posture during the contract negotiation. "Now's our chance," they think, "we'll get a pound of flesh now, because we'll never get the opportunity again." But as any experienced negotiator will attest, an "I win, you lose" mentality is the best way to ensure frustration and begin an unsatisfying relationship. A typical software company is small, and its salespeople most likely talk to its support people. So if you start off having a combative relationship with a salesperson, bad blood might spill over into your support staff relationship, which in the long run can hurt your efforts to get MRP II on the air.

"Wait a moment though," you might say, "doesn't contract negotiation imply some kind of inevitable tug-of-war between customer and vendor?" Not necessarily—the proper course of action is to establish a balanced relationship with the vendor in which *both* parties come out winners. With the possible exceptions of discounts on price, everything in this chapter can be phrased in a manner that protects both parties. In fact, every point that will be negotiated must be based on making the agreement better for everyone. In cases where the warranty and support terms need to be changed, you need to justify why those changes benefit the vendor as well as yourself. Unless you can produce a reasonable, non-confrontational explanation of why the contract should be changed, you shouldn't waste your time in negotiation—just sign the standard contract and get on with implementing MRP II.

In my experience though, there are a number of important aspects of any MRP II software contract that absolutely need to be negotiated. Given the relative infancy of the software business, you should not expect to find the vendor's contract written in a way that adequately protects both parties. Therefore, expect to make changes along the lines of the explanations throughout the chapter.

RULE #2: BE PREPARED

When the time comes to negotiate, you will be under intense pressure because of implementation schedules to sign and have the software delivered, so it's best if you've prepared ahead of time. As early as the evaluation phase, it's worthwhile to get the vendor's standard contract and identify the specific points you wish to negotiate. Waiting until the negotiating session risks delaying the implementation process or being pressured into signing something that is not in your best interest. The simplest remedy is to sort out the contractual issues well in advance and focus on getting a suitable contract written in the shortest possible time.

RULE #3: HAVE THE RIGHT PEOPLE INVOLVED (ON BOTH SIDES)

Besides being prepared, it is vitally important to set up the contract negotiation process so that the individuals doing the negotiating have the authority to sign off. In some cases, the MRP project manager is an excellent choice for doing the negotiating. Other times, the negotiator will be someone from the systems and data processing department. And in some instances, the person may be from purchasing or the finance department. The key issue is not which box on the organizational chart the person hails from, but whether or not the individual understands the objectives of the implementation, has a clear vision of what specific points must be agreed upon, and knows the potential pitfalls of purchasing software. In general, the project manager will meet these criteria; however, as just stated, other people within the company may do just as well.

On the vendor's side, the right person to negotiate the contract may not be the salesperson. Although negotiating with the salesperson is better from your perspective, he or she may not have the authority to agree to all of the points you want to include in the contract, and may end up wasting valuable time waiting for final approval from a superior. The superior may not agree to the terms, in which case the salesperson can become a mere go-between in a drawn out sparring session.

In most cases, the worst people for negotiating software contracts are attorneys. This is not to say that you shouldn't have lawyers involved—your attorney and the vendor's attorney play an important role in ensuring that the language of the contract actually states the agreement between the parties. There is little benefit, however, to writing a dazzling contract that has little to do with effectively installing, maintaining, and operating the software.

RULE #4: DON'T GIVE UP YOUR LEVERAGE

The worst thing you can do is to say to the vendor, "You're the one!" When you do that, you immediately give him two important advantages in conducting his negotiations. First, the knowledge that you've chosen him (and turned off the other vendors) gives him a stronger position and more incentive to take a "hard-line" on some of the points you'd like to change.

The second disadvantage of announcing the winner is that time is on the vendor's side, not yours. Because you are working to meet the deadlines of an aggressive implementation plan, he knows that the rest of your company will be expecting you to quickly wrap up a deal so that the software installation can get under way. For the same reason, you are also at a disadvantage with the other vendor or vendors should your negotiations with vendor Number 1 fall through. They too can bring subtle pressure to bear as they point out how foolish you'll look with your management if you don't finalize the negotiations quickly. In an extreme case you may find the following happening with vendor Number 1 or 2:

As the Paper Mill Turns

Background: You've negotiated a contract with a salesperson. The new version has all the correct language in it to meet your needs. The salesperson says he will have to run it through the bureaucracy at headquarters, and it will take a week or so to get the approvals.

ACT I: THE END OF THE CONTRACT MEETING

The Parting Word (from the salesperson): "No problem getting this baby through—piece of cake!"

ACT II: ONE WEEK LATER

The Telephone Call (from you): "Hi, just calling to check on the contract."

The Response (from the salesperson, as he digs through his in box): "Oh, it's in the works, you know how these bureaucracies are. Call me next week."

ACT III: A WEEK LATER

The Telephone Call (from you, slightly annoyed): "Any status on the contract yet?"

The Response (from the vendor, as he tosses reams of paper out of his in box): "Well as a matter of fact I just checked, and the darn thing is still running in the paper mill—this is an unusually busy time—I promise I'll have something next week."

ACT IV: A WEEK LATER

The Telephone Call (from you, quite annoyed. Senior management has its proverbial heel on your foot): "Hey, what's going on? We've got an implementation to do!"

The Response (from the salesperson, now using a chimney shovel to clear out his in box): "Gosh! I still haven't heard—let me call you back shortly."

AN HOUR LATER . . .

The Telephone Call (from the salesperson, sounding concerned): "Bad news. Still no response, but I get the feeling they're not going to buy it. We better go back over a few points."

The Response (from you, reaching for your Pepto-Bismol): "Everyone around here is ready to tar-and-feather me! What do we have to do to finalize this thing!?"

The Response (to your response): "Well, now that you ask . . ."

Obviously, the preceding dialogue represents an extreme, and it is not meant to imply that many vendors use these tactics. To the contrary, most negotiate honestly and in good faith. It does, however, illustrate what can and sometimes does happen when you give away your leverage. The moral is simple: Give the salesperson a good incentive for wrapping up the deal quickly and fairly, so that you don't walk down the street to a competitor who might give you the decent treatment you deserve.

RULE #5: AVOID STANDARD CONTRACTS WHEN THEY PROTECT ONLY THE VENDOR

Unfortunately, in most situations "standard" software contracts are written as a way to set a negotiating position for the software supplier, rather than as the business agreement that the vendor expects to end up with. Most standard contracts protect the software vendor, without doing much if anything for the licensee's interests.

There are four areas that nearly always need to be renegotiated:

1. *Software specifications.* A typical standard contract states that the software conforms to its own documentation; that is, "The system conforms to the documentation outlined in Volume 1 of the Systems Specification manuals."

Of course, having software that actually works the way it's documented is important, but not primary. For example, there have been several known instances in which a piece of software did not conform to its own documentation, and the customer complained to the vendor. But instead of fixing the system, the vendor changed the documentation!

For someone buying an MRP II system, the important question is: "Does it do MRP II in a normal way?" It is therefore critical to refer to the standard against which the software was evaluated, indicating how the software corresponds to it.

In cases where someone is evaluating MRP software against *The Standard System*, a good method is to state the functional characteristics of the software point-by-point, using specific language such as, "The system includes backscheduling logic that works normally and along the lines of *The Standard System*." If the software does not function according to *The Standard System* and the vendor has committed to the change, the contract must carefully define this responsibility as well as indicate the delivery date. An alternative to the point-by-point format is a reference by exclusion. For example, you might say, "The system includes a set of functions that corresponds to those explained in *The Standard System*, with the exception of . . ."

The technical characteristics would also typically be included in the specifications section of the contract, and would describe such aspects as the operating system (and release level), programming language, TP monitor, data base management system, required system utilities, supported types of disk and tape drives, and other key aspects of the software technology base.

Finally, the specifications section should include a statement of whether the vendor supplied special file conversion or load programs. These programs provide a way to bypass certain sections of system logic, facilitating the initial loading of new files. Although many systems do not provide such programs, they are valuable in reducing the amount of computer time required for file conversions, and any promise of including such programs should be written into the contract.

Obviously, writing any or all of these clauses into a contract affords little protection if the vendor willfully misrepresents his product. The clauses simply raise the plane of any arguments; the issues shift from "whether" and "who" to "when" and "how."

An objective standard is also of benefit to the vendor. After all, if the software does work properly and in accordance with *The Standard System*, it bolsters the vendor's position. The flip side is that most vendors are not going to sign something that says their software performs properly when in fact it doesn't.

Some readers may say, "But we'll never agree. The software supplier will say it works properly, we'll say it doesn't, and we'll be at loggerheads for a long time. How do we avoid this situation?" First, in my experience, this problem doesn't actually happen, so it's something of a groundless fear. Second, companies that are concerned about the possibility of locking horns with a vendor should specify an arbitrator. In most cases, a company will be using outside consulting support to help get MRP II up and running. That person may also turn out to be the best choice as a final arbitrator of disputes.

2. *Payment terms.* The second reason for avoiding standard contracts concerns payments. Many vendors preprint their contracts with a payment schedule stating that 90 percent will be paid on

signing the contract and the balance on delivery, or 75 percent will be paid on signing, one percent on delivery, and the balance on acceptance.

Neither of these payment plans is fair or acceptable, based on the following simple test of reasonableness: what major purchases does anyone make during their lifetime where there is no benefit from the purchase for a year or more? An automobile? Certainly not—the buyer of a new car can drive it off the lot. A house? Again no—you can move in after passing papers. About the only things that people purchase that do not offer immediate use and benefits are life insurance and cemetery plots.

Given the absurdity of paying 90 percent up front for MRP II software, you should hope that the vendor suggests you sign a contract with such terms; it is so extreme that he is clearly sending the message "I'm willing to negotiate." And he will.

From the buyer's perspective, a revised payment plan will reduce the amount of red ink at the beginning of the MRP II implementation by spreading the payments over a longer period. For some companies, this may make the funding of the MRP implementation easier. As an example of changes that are sometimes made to the software payment schedule, consider the following schedule:

— 10 percent down (on contract signing).
— 10 percent on completion of a vendor-supplied acceptance test.
— 10 percent tied to testing of data you developed.
— 10 percent upon completion of a volume test.
— The balance paid every few months across the remainder of the implementation. (See Figure 7.1 for a list of other cost-related issues that should be spelled out in the contract.)

With this schedule, total payments would be made within a year. The vendor might want to charge interest at the current rate, which is a reasonable concession for you to make (obviously don't bring up the idea yourself). If the vendor suggests going to a finance company or borrowing from a bank, however, stand your ground. The reason is that if the software does not function properly, or if the vendor fails to meet his obligations or goes belly

QUESTIONS:

- Cost of fully operational product?
- Downpayment?
- Due on delivery?
- Due on acceptance?
- Due on volume test?
- Due on implementation?
- What options? At what price?
- Discounts for second/third sites?
- Cost of installation/training?
- Customization fees?

- Documentation fees?
- Consulting rates?
- Who pays for travel time/report writing?
- Additional fees?
- On-going maintenance (% and basis)?
- Replacement costs?
- Maintenance covers fixes only, or fixes and enhancements?
- Upgrade fee if maintenance lapses?

Figure 7.1
Cost-related issues for a software contract

up, leaving you in the lurch, you still have to pay the finance company. Worse, you've given up your only real leverage with the vendor: the purse strings.

3. *Reasonable amounts of support.* The third reason to avoid standard contracts is that most do not specify the "ground rules" for support. If you played touch football as a kid, you remember how it was always better to define the goal lines and out-of-bounds line before the first play. Doing so tended to cut down the number of arguments and black eyes.

The same holds true with a software warranty—you have to decide the boundaries before you start playing. That means defining various categories of problems, and the type of response that the vendor must make for each one.

Lower level bugs might be classified as those problems that are a nuisance, but can be tolerated if a workaround is in place. While such situations may not be ideal, it is not necessary or realistic to insist that the vendor drop everything and rush out a correction. An example of a minor bug would be a printed MRP report that has some extraneous characters displayed in the descriptive information. Another would be a situation in which a low volume transaction does not work reliably, but two other transactions run back-to-back will achieve the same function. In each case, the system can still be used, and progress with MRP II is still possible.

More significant bugs are those that cause you to stop making progress with MRP. A problem causing gross requirements to be calculated incorrectly, for example, would prevent you from running MRP. If the software causes a hard halt and a core dump every Tuesday at 10 AM and you cannot get it back up and running until the following Thursday, you'll certainly have your progress slowed. These kinds of problems would require immediate attention from the vendor, and the vendor's responsibility should be outlined in the contract.

Gil Tatman, a top systems professional from Cessna Aircraft Corporation and a former IBM systems engineer, suggests that contract language specifying response to software problems could be patterned after similar language in IBM's hardware contracts. For most companies, this would be an excellent place to start.

Language for minor problems will probably just state that the vendor is responsible for fixing the problem within some time frame, say 90 days. Language for serious bugs might include concepts such as "the vendor has two days in which to respond with the fix by local support people. If the local people do not respond with a fix within that period, then we have access to the national support group, which then has two days to fix the problem. If they do not fix the problem within two days, then your support group must pay a site visit and remain on site until the problem is resolved."

In some cases a software vendor will counter the suggestion that this kind of support be provided by saying: "We have a well-tested piece of software, and our experience shows that most really serious bugs develop as a result of software modifications that users make." Your response? "We will be happy to reimburse your company for travel and expenses, as well as labor at consulting rates for whatever time is spent if it turns out that we caused the problem." From the vendor's perspective this is a nearly risk-free proposition, and a major benefit is that it properly ranks the systems and data processing work that needs to be done to support customers.

4. *Agreements on violation of warranty.* The last reason to rewrite standard contracts is because they generally state that any modifications of the source code will void the warranty. This is unrealistic, because as we've stressed throughout this book, *all* MRP II software requires some modifications. On the other hand, it is also unrealistic to say that a vendor must continue to support the software if you change 90 percent of the source code. What is needed is a set of guidelines for the kinds of changes that can be made without losing the vendor's support obligation.

Such guidelines might include statements like, "We will attempt to make functional changes to the program externally, through subroutines and our own programs that are easily documented and identified whenever possible. If it is necessary to modify the source code to perform a function efficiently, or if it is impossible to perform a function without making changes to the source code, the changes will be clearly documented and identified for the vendor's inspection."

As long as the guidelines are reasonable, the vendor should have no trouble accepting them. After all, as discussed above in Section 3, since you're willing to reimburse the vendor for errors caused by your alterations, the vendor is really taking very little risk.

RULE #6: BEWARE OPEN-ENDED LANGUAGE

A contract written in open-ended language may not be much of a contract at all; the whole point of a contract is to pin down terms, obligations, and recourses as tightly as possible. Regardless, there are dozens of software companies and users who fall prey to open language every year.

Some open-ended statements are obvious: " . . . at some mutually agreed upon future date we will develop a government contract reporting module to the specifications provided by . . . '' Other open-ended statements are not as obvious: ''When the DB2 version of the software package is released, you will receive a copy at no additional charge.''

In the first example, the problem is the phrase ''mutually agreed upon future date.'' The only time it's likely that you'll get a mutually agreed upon date is before the contract is signed.

In the second example, the situation is partly clear. If there ever is a DB2 version, you will get it for free. But while it sounds like the vendor is making a commitment to developing a DB2 version, there is no obligation for him to do so. The ''when'' in the statement should really read *''if and when it becomes available.''* Many companies have bought software on the basis of an open-ended ''when'' statement, thinking that the vendor has made a commitment to a particular operating system, data base management system, CPU, or TP monitor, when in fact the contract does not say so at all.

RULE #7: IF IT ISN'T WRITTEN DOWN, IT ISN'T PART OF THE DEAL

Verbal contracts, as Samuel Goldwyn so eloquently described, may not be worth much when there are disputes or problems. Of course, you don't need to transcribe every conversation that you ever had with a vendor. But if you expect special pricing in the future, discounts on later versions, or special service because your company is a beta test site, write those expectations into the contract.

This rule is important, because salespeople do move around in the industry, and those whom you deal with today may not be at the software company tomorrow. How convincing can you be with the argument that ''your predecessor or former salesman said we could have X,Y and Z for free''?

In addition to documenting promises for service, updates, and discounts, any correspondence with the vendor or written responses to proposals in which the vendor has made claims about the functionality of the software should be included as contract addenda.

RULE #8: DISTINGUISH NEGOTIABLE AND NON-NEGOTIABLE POINTS

If you observe the rules in this chapter, negotiating your contract will be a positive experience for both you and the vendor, and will likely leave you with the satisfaction of having created a win-win situation. Do not, however, assume that everything on the table can be negotiated back and forth. Two items are cast in stone, so do not waste your time trying to chip them away:

1. *Ownership.* Software contracts are normally a license for use on a CPU or CPUs, not the sale and transfer of ownership of the software. While you may typically use the software "in perpetuity," the vendor actually owns it, and it is unlikely he will ever give up his ownership rights.

A somewhat related ownership question revolves around the ownership of custom-developed software where you paid for the development but the vendor did the work. In most cases the vendor can argue that there were a number of design choices, that not all the work was done under your direct supervision, and therefore the software that resulted from his effort is his property. In fact, unless you have negotiated a contract that states something to the contrary, most courts will rule in the developer's favor. Consequently, if you are paying for extensive development or modifications, you must specify in the contract what portion you own.

In cases where you retain the ownership rights to custom software, you may choose to allow the software supplier to market the software changes in return for some sort of royalty. This royalty may take the form of payments to your company, or credits against the purchase of additional software from the vendor. It may be capped at some fixed amount (say the total development cost) or some number of years (say 10 years following the completion of the changes), or it may go on forever. All such arrangements must be spelled out in black and white beforehand. Once the die is cast, it will be very difficult to change the rules of the game.

2. *Copyright, patent, and indemnity.* These clauses say that you will be held harmless in the event that the vendor violated copyright or patent law in creating his MRP II package. This paragraph is designed to protect you, and assuming that your attorney has OK'd the language, it should not be changed. A semi-negotiable point concerns the confidentiality of the documentation. All vendors will include a statement that says you will hold his materials in confidence, and that you will not release his documentation to anyone else outside your company. Sometimes this point can get a little sticky, because the language will say that you will hold the documentation in the same confidence that you will hold your other business secrets. If you are a major soft drink manufacturer with a 100-year-old secret formula, you will go to great lengths and expense to protect your trade secrets. But you won't even consider instituting the same costly security measures to ensure that a vendor's instruction manual doesn't get seen by unauthorized eyes. So, while the issue of confidentiality will surely have to be addressed, you may wish to alter the specifics of the language in the vendor's standard contract.

Another contract clause that may be somewhat negotiable is one that enables you to show the software documentation to a third party consultant. One possibility is for the vendor to add a non-disclosure statement that extends the confidentiality agreement to people whom you retain or hire as outside experts. This can be important, because if you do run into trouble down line and want additional expert help, the consultant may wish to examine the documentation to make a recommendation.

RULE #9: USE A DEFERRED PAYMENT AS A PERFORMANCE PENALTY (WHEN APPROPRIATE)

In many industries, performance penalties are a normal part of doing business. When major airplane manufacturers take contracts for planes that are being developed, they generally commit themselves to a series of performance standards and penalties for late deliveries. Software vendors should be equally accountable and liable for their failures to deliver.

The most effective way to write a performance penalty is in the form of a deferred payment, rather than a fine. The deferred payment gives the vendor an incentive to work hard and collect his money; the fine takes money out of his pocket, and is therefore less acceptable.

An example of a deferred payment plan might occur in the following situation: a company is purchasing an MRP II system in which the capacity requirements planning system is still under development. There are other software alternatives but the company feels that the vendor it chose has a superior technical solution and is worth the risk. In addition, a Plan B is in place so that if the vendor fails to deliver, the company can write its own CRP system.

In this situation, the company might offer to defer some portion of the payment on the material requirements planning and master production scheduling software until after the CRP module is delivered. For example, they might choose to pay 50 percent up front, and the remaining 50 percent plus the license fee for CRP upon delivery of the capacity requirements planning system. This kind of payment plan gives the vendor a strong incentive to finish as soon as possible.

Performance penalties should be structured so that the deferred payment is written off forever if the vendor misses the date, and should not be tied to a delivery of the software at any point in the future. The West Company learned this the hard way when it bought a new $100,000 general ledger system from a well-known supplier, and put in an order for the accounts payable package. Since the A/P package would not be ready until the following year, West wisely deferred a payment totaling $50,000 (the license fee of the A/P package plus a portion of the general ledger license).

Unfortunately, West did not specify in its contract that failure to meet the deadline released it from any obligation to pay the balance. The vendor took nearly three years to complete the A/P program, during which time West wrote its own system and implemented it. When the vendor finally delivered the software to West, it demanded the license fee for the payables software plus the deferred balance on the general ledger, according to the (open-ended) terms of the contract.

As you can imagine, West was less than enthusiastic about paying $50,000 for a program that it neither needed nor wanted and that was three years late. At this moment, the two companies are still wrangling over the outcome.

Consequently, the proper way to write a performance penalty is to specify delivery on or before a particular date. If the vendor misses the date, the payment is waived, Also, make sure there is an acceptance test in the contract, so that the vendor cannot deliver useless code just to make a delivery date.

And what if the vendor won't agree to such performance penalties? In my experience, this means he already knows he'll miss the date. Either forget him, or plan on developing this software yourself from the start.

RULE #10: PROVIDE FOR ADEQUATE TEST PERIODS

The contract should allow enough time for testing the software both against the vendor's data and your own data. There should be some statement that if the software fails the acceptance test, the vendors will have the opportunity to correct it before you exercise any of your options under the contract. There should also be a definable limit on how long the vendor has to make the fixes. When you buy a new piece of software, it is especially important to make sure there is an escape clause that provides a way for you to get out of the contract altogether.

RULE #11: NEGOTIATE A SOUND MAINTENANCE CONTRACT

Software maintenance contracts normally are designed to extend the warranty period from the first year. Normally this extension is done in yearly increments for eight to 15 percent of the purchase price, the then-current price, the best customer price, or some other acceptable price. The maintenance contract usually covers the full range of services provided under the warranty program. There are some vendors, however, who do not offer such coverage, so an informed buyer should check to see whether the maintenance contract covers fixes only, or fixes and enhancements.

One other key part of the maintenance contract negotiation is the length of time you commit yourself to taking maintenance versus the length of time the vendor is obligated to offer it. As a responsible user, you will need to determine the value of continued maintenance each year. After all, you'll likely be paying anywhere from ten thousand to eighty thousand dollars per year for software maintenance. Someday your boss will undoubtedly ask, "What is it that we get for all this money?"

While you want the option of not signing a maintenance contract, you always want the software vendor to be obligated to provide a "window of maintenance." The window helps guarantee that your own people are capable of supporting the package if the vendor drops the system. For this reason, most companies purchasing MRP II software should insist on a window of maintenance of at least 24 months. In most cases this provides enough time to learn how to support the system internally or to make alternate plans with another support organization.

Either the maintenance contract or the license agreement should provide a way to restart maintenance if it has lapsed for some time. Let's say you decide to drop maintenance because the fixes and improvements don't justify the expense. Several years later, the software supplier releases a new version that has some functional or technological advantages. As a result, you may wish to obtain the new version without relicensing the system for the full purchase price. To provide for this situation, you should write a contract clause that allows maintenance to restart simply by paying the missed maintenance fees (one year's maintenance, two years' maintenance, etc.) or the missed fees plus interest.

Finally, it's essential to verify that you're not obligated to sign up for maintenance in order to continue using the software. One major vendor requires users to pay an initial $800,000 for use of software, and a maintenance fee of $80,000 a year for each year they use it. In this case, if a client company chooses not to pay the $80,000 yearly license, they are not legally permitted to continue operating the system.

In my opinion, any company that spends $800,000 for a piece of software should be able to use it forever without additional charge. Whether you want maintenance support is a separate issue. In any case, the range of cost on the maintenance contract is typically 8 to 15 percent of the purchase price.

SPECIAL CASE: OBJECT CODE ONLY SOFTWARE CONTRACTS

As mentioned in Chapter 6, object code only software is becoming more common in MRP II software packages, and raises some unique contractual issues. A contract for object code only software must clearly spell out the level of support the vendor will provide, and must include a description of the functions in the system with a statement from the vendor that they work in the normal way with regard to *The Standard System*. It should also contain provisions under which the source code will be surrendered to the user if missing functions are not added, if needed modifications are not made, or if the vendor chooses to go out of the MRP software business (voluntarily or through a bankruptcy filing). In addition, the contract should contain a clear statement that the software is stored in an escrow account, and should name the individual or organization that is responsible for the account.

Finally, potential users of object code only software should be wary of purchasing the software from third parties unless the third parties have the source code. If they do not have the source code, third parties will merely function as buffers or middlemen between a customer and the vendor. And that is the last situation you want to be in when trying to resolve serious deficiencies and problems with the software.

To one degree or another, all of these issues revolve around a larger issue of accountability. Who is accountable for object code only software? The vendor? The systems and data processing department of the customer? The customer's implementation team? The ultimate answer is simple: in the end, the data processing manager and his people must be accountable for making the system work on the company's computer. With any MRP II software acquisition, the data processing manager and his technical staff are responsible for modifying the package to make it work. In the case of object code only MRP II software, the data processing manager is really just subcontracting the software development and maintenance to the vendor, and he is still accountable for the results. The bottom line is that a data processing manager should be free to use object code only software if he is confident in the vendor's ability to support it and make the necessary changes. It's his choice. It's also his job.

SUMMARY

- Avoid an adversarial relationship in contract negotiations. If you go in looking to do battle and squeeze the vendor dry, you are unlikely to get what you need or want.
- Be prepared—look at the vendors' contracts as early as possible in the software evaluation phase.
- Never sign a standard contract unless it provides you with the proper protection; whenever possible use the standard against which you evaluated the software as the functional specification for the system.
- Make the payment schedule make sense—don't give up the financial leverage you have with the vendor.
- Incorporate in the contract the kinds of responses that a vendor must provide for various kinds of bugs. Major bugs that prevent progress with MRP II must be dealt with swiftly and effectively.
- Avoid open-ended language. Be specific about dates and obligations.
- If it isn't written down, it isn't part of the deal. Every major point that you and the vendor agree upon must be specifically stated in writing.
- If you include performance penalties in your contract, structure them in a way that you defer partial payment on other software delivery of the new code, and if the deadline is missed, the remaining payment is waived.
- Only accept maintenance contracts that can be bought one year at a time. Use the first year as a trial period to determine whether it's worth the expense.
- Be sure the vendor is obligated to a "window of maintenance"—don't get caught without sufficient time to train your resident systems and programming group to support the system.

Chapter 8

Putting It All Together:

Installing the System

*How to fold a diaper depends on the size of the baby
and the diaper.*
(Dr. Benjamin Spock, pediatrician)

Some systems and data processing people assume that once the user education is done and the MRP II software has been selected, the internal systems and data processing work is finished and the "package, guided by the supplier," takes over. But as you've probably come to expect from this book, the bad news is that the hard work is far from over. First of all, you may have looked at a variety of alternatives and decided not to use packaged software at all. In other words, you may have determined that upgrading the existing system was the "least worst choice." In this situation, you probably have made some effort, maybe a significant one, to make the system conform to *The Standard System*. Conversely, you may have decided that the best alternative is packaged software, in which case you must worry about installation, verification, modification, conversion, interfacing, and other important issues.

The task at hand is to make sure that the software performs in a normal manner and along the lines of the explanation in *The Standard System*. In the case of homegrown software that's being upgraded, this effort is probably in development; in the case of packaged software, it's a matter of verifying that the software conforms in the manner described in the contract, and that it actually can be interfaced to existing systems or converted mechanically from systems that are being replaced. The following topics require careful attention to ensure that you will get the MRP II software on the air as quickly as possible without impeding the overall implementation efforts.

TRAINING FROM THE VENDOR

Training on the software package is essential to operating the system, but it shouldn't be confused with general education (behavior modification) on the principles of MRP II. General education, done properly, covers the concepts and principles of MRP II, so that users understand why and how an MRP II system works at a detailed level. The general educational process also helps users develop a sense of how the business will be run using the tools of MRP II. Software training from the vendor covers specific forms, transactions, reports, data elements, and program logic in the system. The later phases of the implementation, the conference room and live pilots, verify that the education and software training were done properly, and that it's okay to "go live." General education is flight school, training is flying in a simulator, the conference room pilot is flying with an instructor, and the live pilot is going solo.

Everyone must do training. The degree to which you use the vendor's training program depends on the amount of time you have. In most cases, companies following an aggressive implementation schedule like the one in Appendix D will choose to use the vendor's training program because the alternative (developing the initial training materials) is so time consuming. At some point, however, a company must reach the masses of people who'll use the system and provide training on the specific forms, transactions, and reports that are part of the system. Typically, this training process is integrated with the general MRP II education, so that after discussing the concepts and principles of MRP II and getting into the specifics of how to run the company with the tools of MRP II, a company can understand the mechanics (reports, transactions, and other features) of the system.

From a systems and data processing perspective, it's essential to understand the architecture of the system, points of interface, and other technical aspects. Although one or more DP people will have been involved in the investigation and evaluation of the software, and will be part of the team that makes the necessary changes and develops the interfaces, there will probably be additional people who will be helping in the technical part of the implementation. These people probably need to go outside to the vendor's training on the "internals" of the system, so that they can begin the technical part of the installation. This should happen immediately after contract signing or, if possible, during the final stages of the evaluation process.

INSTALLATION

The amount of time required to install a complete MRP II software package on the computer may range from an hour or two to well over three weeks. Several factors affect the amount of time required, including:

1. Whether a vendor training class is required prior to the delivery of installation materials.
2. The physical media of the installation materials, and who is responsible for installing the package on the computer.
3. Whether or not the software supplier delivers object code that can be link-edited, or whether the system must be compiled from the source code.
4. Your company's policies on the installation of software, specifically, whether you normally link-edit vendor supplied object modules, or whether the software must be compiled from source.
5. The amount of time required to verify the software installation occurred properly.

In the case of mainframe software, attending software vendor training may be prerequisite to any software installation. In the case of several software suppliers a three to five day installation course covers the topics necessary to bring up the software on the client company's computer: how to modify JCL and set systems options and control records; how to run the standard test sequence and verify the software against test or sample output; and how to install updates, upgrades, and future maintenance releases. Class attendees leave with documentation manuals and the installation tape under their arm.

The second issue affecting installation time is the physical media on which the software is delivered. You'll need to verify that the vendor will supply installation materials that are compatible with your computer, or else provide an alternate method for loading the software into your machine. For example, if you have an IBM System/38 computer with a diskette magazine but no tape drive, you'll need to rent machine time somewhere if the vendor supplies his software on magnetic tape. In addition, you'll probably need to plan on having a block of time available for the installer, who may be one of your own people or one of the vendor's people.

The third issue affecting installation, particularly for users of mainframe computers, is whether the software is delivered as object code that can be link-edited, or source code that has to be compiled and then link-edited. Clearly, compiling and link-editing an MRP II system of one million source statements will take significantly longer than link-editing the same system. Just finding blocks of computer time to do the compilation may be a significant problem in this case, since a mainframe MRP II package might require more than two weeks to compile and link.

In addition, it may be your company's policy to compile from the source code, even when the object modules are available. The advantage of working from the source code is that you can trace any problems back to it. If you just link-edit the object code, and a problem arises, you have no guarantee that it is related to the source code, and could waste hours chasing down the cause. As noted before, though, if you do have to compile from the source code, be prepared to spend a significant amount of time on the installation.

Regardless of all the above considerations, the vendor should provide a standard test sequence that can be run to make sure the programs generate the anticipated results. This is done by comparing the output on vendor-supplied data with correct results provided by the vendor. Many vendors provide client companies with actual printouts or photocopies of printouts to show what the reports should look like. In the case of some vendors who require attendance at an installation course, the class attendees may actually install the software in a private account on the software vendor's computer, generate standard test results, and verify the output against the software vendor's standard results. Upon completion of the course, each class attendee has both the installation tape and a set of standard output that can be used for verification (the test output from the class, once verified, becomes the standard output for the installation at the client site).

The importance of having standard test output is underscored by an experience from my early days at Software International, a pioneer in the MRP II software marketplace. One of our first client companies had installed its own software, and because there had been no hard halts or obvious problems in the installation process, it had not thoroughly checked the installation output against the standard test output supplied by SI. Unfortunately for the client company, several of the object modules supplied in the distribution material were from a development library and not from the current installation library. Consequently, for the following six weeks, the system generated a number of strange errors, hard halts, and core dumps that absolutely baffled the technical people at both the client company and the main support people in Andover, Massachusetts. It wasn't until all other possibilities had been eliminated, and the client company was forced to re-review the output from the installation procedure, that we determined there had been installation problems.

Who was at fault? In fact, both parties have to share the blame in this example. Software International failed to fulfill its quality control obligations—it supplied the wrong software modules. The customer failed to fulfill its installation responsibilities—it failed to check the installation output against the standard output.

Regardless of where the blame falls, though, the incident delivers an important message: insist that the software supplier provide some method of verifying the installation process. Don't just assume that if the software transferred from the installation tape to your computer it will work properly. And having insisted that the software supplier provide a standard installation test, make sure you check the output against the standard.

ACCEPTANCE TESTING

Once the software has been installed and verified using the vendor's standard test sequence, the next step should be an acceptance test run using your own data. Acceptance testing is best done by creating standard test files, which comprise a working model of your live data base. These standard test files can also be used later as a way to test future releases of the system, and as a test bed for system modifications, improvements, and interfaces.

The standard test files should include actual company part numbers, bill of materials, shop and purchase orders, control file options that you use, and whatever data elements are necessary to simulate the operation of the system in your company. Since it is physically impossible to test every combination of codes, switches, and options (you would never get to the point of actually using the system), your test system must be a valid simulation of your operating environment. It's the vendor's responsibility to test the other combinations and permutations of codes, switches, and various options.

So, in addition to containing data elements and switch settings for the way your company operates the master production schedule, material requirements plan, shop schedule, capacity plan and other functions, the test system should include a series of standard transactions that can be run as a way to verify or validate changes and enhancements to the system. For example, the test system might include a series of standard inventory transactions that would be run whenever changes are made to programs in the inventory transaction system, and a set of standard bill of material transactions for testing modifications to the bill of material system. These transactions may be batch transactions, or a script of transactions that have to be entered using the on-line system.

"But," you might ask, "why not just test the system with the vendor's test data, and after you are up and running with MRP II, test various modifications and new releases against the production data base or a copy of the production data base. Why go to the bother of creating new files, transactions, etc?" There are several answers.

First, it's risky business to accept a system on the basis of what is typically a small amount of vendor testing. A typical MRP II software package has so many combinations and permutations of options that the software vendor cannot possibly test every one. Instead, the vendor tests what he considers the "normal" options, releasing the system to his users and letting them test the rest of the options under live conditions. Provided your company's options fall within the set of "normal" options, you're probably okay. If not, there could be difficulties that make the MRP II implementation a hostage to software problems. In addition, what data processing professional hasn't had a phone call like the following:

Hold That Tape, Please

DP PROFESSIONAL: "Hello, Karen Volney here."

VENDOR SUPPORT PERSON: "Hi, Karen, this is Bill Wilson calling from the Acme Software Company. I'm calling to see if you've received our distribution tape for the new release."

DP PROFESSIONAL: "Yes, Bill, as a matter of fact we have, got it the day before yesterday."

VENDOR SUPPORT PERSON (sounding concerned): "You . . . you haven't installed it yet, have you?"

DP PROFESSIONAL: "Gee, no, Bill. We were thinking about getting a block of time in the next few days so we can bring it up. After all, there may be some real key improvements that our users will want to start taking advantage of."

VENDOR SUPPORT PERSON (relieved): "Well, ah, just wait a couple of days, will you? There turned out to be a few problems in the new release that got caught by the first few users, ah I mean, well the first companies that put it up . . . and ah, well we'll be sending out a new tape in the next few days. No sense loading the system and taking the time when you may have some problems and you'll have to do it over again later."

Aside from the possibility of getting an annoying call from old Bill from the vendor's technical support office, running acceptance tests on new releases and modifications against a full-sized data base is impractical if not impossible. As many systems and data processing professionals find out early in their careers, using the whole data base for an acceptance test can commit you to working evenings, nights, early mornings, and weekends, since it may require many more hours of computer time than the company can afford to relinquish during normal working hours. A test on a copy of the live data base will also generate massive amounts of paper, and the additional volume of paper may not make problem identification simpler.

Although testing against live files under live conditions won't win anyone the title "Data Processing Professional of the Year," there are always individuals who feel that this is an acceptable way to install and check out changes. "After all, I made the changes myself, and I'm very thorough. There's less than a five percent chance there will be any problems."

Regardless of the risk of problems, the stakes involved in testing under live conditions are too high for this to be an acceptable operating procedure. Few companies that I've been involved with can afford to have its information systems shut down for one or more days when there is a problem. And no rational manager will risk his operating results for the sake of having a few software improvements working a few days earlier at best. Don't even consider taking this course of action; if you do, you deserve the consequences.

VOLUME TESTING AND TUNING

Volume testing is the flip side of acceptance testing. The idea is to create full-sized test files (the same number of items, bills of material, purchase orders, and other elements that will be in the live data base) and determine how long it takes the system to run the major batch functions that are being implemented. These batch functions typically include the master production schedule, material requirements plan, capacity requirements plan, etc.

The purpose of volume tests is to verify that run times are within acceptable ranges for operating the system on an on-going basis. If run times have been stipulated in the contract, the volume tests should help identify problems enough in advance to get the vendor's assistance in resolving the problem. If run times have not been stipulated in the contract, then it will be your responsibility to tune the system and bring the run times down to acceptable ranges of time.

The Smith and Jones Company discovered the problems of inadequate volume testing when it installed its software and was amazed to discover that the first material requirements planning run required 120 hours of processing time! In successive runs it was able to improve the system performance, dropping MRP run times to 70 hours. Unfortunately, the company was not able to dedicate its mainframe computer to this processing. But even if it were, at 70 hours of MRP processing time it wouldn't have been realistic to run MRP even once a week.

The solution to run time problems, as Smith and Jones discovered, is judicious tuning. The company first reviewed buffer sizes and blocking factors, gaining some significant improvements through changes here. In the second phase of tuning, programming modifications were identified that cut run times significantly. In all, run times were cut more than 50 percent through intelligent tuning. Still, the tuning took time and the implementation and operation of MRP II were sidetracked unnecessarily. All in all, the lack of volume testing probably cost Smith and Jones a year or more in getting MRP on the air—a powerful argument for doing volume testing under test, not live, conditions.

Tuning is also an on-going responsibility of the systems and data processing department, and should be part of a yearly system audit. Software tuning activities run the gamut from simple tasks to high level system analysis. An example of the former would be what gave Smith and Jones a big boost—changing the blocking factors and buffer sizes so that you get an optimal number of records being read from the data base at any given time and keeping them in main memory. Another simple tuning activity involves putting different files on different disks to minimize head contention. For instance, it may be possible to optimize MRP run times by putting the bill of material file on a different drive from the planned order and pegging files.

A more complex tuning action would be rewriting portions of the software so they run more efficiently. A Big Eight consulting firm, Arthur Andersen, claimed that by rewriting part of a popular mainframe package, it had been able to reduce MRP run times, under actual client conditions, by one third. In my own experience, a client company who recently redesigned their homegrown software projects a conservative one third reduction in MRP run time and a 50 percent reduction in data base accesses in the on-line MRP-related transactions, which gives you a sense of the dramatic performance improvements that can be realized by a well-executed rewrite. It should also be said that these performance improvements were gained without loss of functionality.

POST INSTALLATION ACTIVITIES

Once the installation tests are complete, there are a number of important activities to be performed. Conversion programs can be written, necessary modifications (the ones identified in the evaluation process) can be made, and control file options must be set. Also, both temporary and permanent interfaces will have to be built.

Conversion

For companies converting from an automated system to a piece of packaged software, a key step in the process is a "data element review." This entails comparing the data needed to run the new system with the data available from the old system, and vice versa. The field names, field sizes, and in some cases even the field characteristics will not be the same, so someone will have to map the data from the old system to the new system. In most cases this must be done field by field by field. For example, the old system may have a field called the "item type," which is defined as a single character alphabetic code, where "A" means finished goods; "B," subassembly; "C," fabrication; "D," weldment; "E," purchased part; and "F," raw material. The new system may have a similar code, called the part status, that is two digits, where "10" means finished goods; "20," subassembly; "30," fabrication; "40," raw material; and "50," purchased part. So "A" maps to code "10," "B" to "20," "C" and "D" to "30," "E" to "50," and "F" to "40." This one-to-one mapping is necessary before any conversion or interface programming can be done.

It may also be the case that information stored in the old system in one file may not be stored in the corresponding file in the new system. For example, the existing system may have a file, the item master file, that stores both the descriptive information about the item but also up to four inventory locations and the balance on hand in each location. Further, suppose that the new system provides an unlimited number of inventory locations by providing an inventory location file that is separate from the item master information in the system. In this situation, someone will have to map the item information from one item master to the other, and map the location and on-hand balance information from the item master file (old system) to the location file (new system).

Once data elements and files have been mapped from the old system to the new, conversion programs can be written. Typically these take the form of "strip and load" programs, where one program strips data from the old files and converts the data elements into the corresponding fields in the new software. Transactions are typically written to a batch file that can be processed later to load the new system.

Control File Settings

Another activity that follows installation involves setting up control fields for the new system, prerequisite to which may be attendance in the vendor's training classes. Control file information may include elements such as date format (European or U.S.); the value for inspection lead time (the normal time required for items that require incoming inspection); and the order closure time (the amount of time that a closed order will remain on file before it is purged).

Since control files have global impact, the way they are set up should not be left up to the sole discretion of the systems or data processing department. In most cases, the decision on the individual control file elements is made by the project team, perhaps with the assistance of their MRP counsel and the software support person.

Program Modifications

At this point, program modifications should also be started. Generally, these program changes should be limited to the ones identified in the software evaluation and where the lack of the function will cause a serious risk to the MRP II implementation. In other words, there's lots of other work to do without looking for unnecessary changes to the system.

Before the work commences, it is important to get the entire project team to agree on what modifications will be made and how they are to be accomplished. If the end users are left out of the decision making process, or the systems group is allowed to make modifications for them, everyone may be in for an unpleasant surprise. In some cases, this will be because the systems and data processing departments will do more than required (but take forever to do it). The fact that no one appreciates the extra work they undertook at their own initiative will probably cause more than one of the systems and DP people to be disgruntled. On the other hand, there will be other cases where the data processing department acted in a vacuum and created modifications that are unusable to the rest of the organization. Because the changes are unusable, they may actually hinder the operation of MRP. And of course nothing is more likely to invoke the wrath of the project manager and other users.

Temporary Interfaces

As in the case of program modifications, temporary interfaces were probably mapped out sometime during the evaluation phase. At this point, however, some people will probably get impatient and try to convince the project team that it's better to accelerate the implementation of MRP than to write the throwaway code necessary to keep the old ordering system running. It is safe to say that in *all* cases this would be a major mistake, and is a virtual guarantee that you will not only risk your MRP implementation, but will also make things worse with respect to getting shipments out the door.

It is absolutely essential that you continue to run the business during the time that MRP II is being implemented. To do this you must continue to order material using the old system(s). To do otherwise is equivalent to an unplanned "cold-turkey" cutover, which is an experience that most companies would rather not re-live.

Take the case of paper manufacturer Balcon Corp., whose DP department thought it would be too much effort to write all those temporary interfaces after it installed its new, state-of-the-art mainframe MRP II package. At the same time, the DP staff felt they could not continue to stay on the old inventory system, because "the old inventory transaction system was preventing us from getting accurate inventory records." Sadly for Balcon, the MRP II project team convinced themselves that "it can't be worse than it is today," and (unbeknownst to the rest of the people in the company) authorized the systems and data processing department to cutover the inventory system one weekend *without having the temporary interfaces to drive the old ordering system!*

On the following Monday, there was no way to order material using the old systems and procedures, and since no one was far enough along in their understanding of MRP, an attempt to get the planners to order using MRP turned into a fiasco. Not a soul in the company was prepared for the cutover and to add insult to injury, a number of response time problems started to appear. The effects were so damaging that the company's productivity began flagging, and shipments started to drop, causing its stock to tumble. The episode even earned Balcon the dubious honor of being written up in the nation's leading business tabloid in a scathing article that explained how the decline of the once-profitable company coincided with the installation of a newfangled computer system. In fact, the problems had more to do with dubious management decisions (the cold turkey cutover) and laziness (the fact that data processing didn't want to write the throwaway interfaces) than it did with the implementation of MRP II.

As important as temporary interfaces are, many companies, especially larger ones, tend to pay lip service to them during the planning phase. "Oh, we'll get there somehow," is a prevalent attitude among systems and data processing people in big firms. Unfortunately, the only way to get from here to there is with a good map and small bridges. Giant steps might be great for the first walk on the moon, but they spell disaster for an MRP installation.

Permanent Interfaces

Permanent interfaces must also be identified during the planning phase. Examples of permanent interfaces include the interface between purchasing and payables for invoice matching, the interface between the order entry system and the master production schedule, the interface between the inventory accounting system and the inventory transaction system. Eventually, all of these interfaces will probably be built. What is important to remember, though, is that a company seeking the tremendous benefits from MRP should not delày those benefits until all the interfaces have been built. In the examples above, the only truly essential interface is the one between the order entry system and the master production schedule, so customer demands can be shown in the master production schedule display, and so the master production schedule can be managed effectively.

Computer (Data Processing) Pilot and the Conference Room Pilot

The Computer Pilot (sometimes called the Data Processing Pilot) encompasses the acceptance testing process described earlier. Some portion of the volume testing activity may also be included in the Computer Pilot, although in most companies, the project team would be willing to proceed with other phases of the implementation as soon as the acceptance test is complete. Consequently, volume testing often occurs concurrently with the "Conference Room Pilot" that is being done for the users.

The objective of the Computer Pilot is to verify the correct operation of the software. In the case of "homegrown" software, this involves testing and debugging, although packaged software requires testing and debugging, too. In each case, people from systems and data processing plus a few key members of the project team should be involved.

Once the software has passed the test of the Computer Pilot, the project should move to the Conference Room Pilot phase. While it is not live, the Conference Room Pilot is a functionally complete replica of the actual system. It will be used anywhere from two to six weeks, and has several important functions.

First, it will be used in teaching the users how the system works and verifying that they understand the specific details of the system. Second, it is the last chance to shake down the system prior to going live. To achieve both of these purposes, the software must be as complete as possible. In the first case, completeness is important so users can verify their normal operating procedures. In the second case, it is important because the software must be complete and reliable *before* the pilot begins; be assured that there is no greater way to shake the confidence of users than to change the software as they are trying to operate in live conditions.

SUMMARY

- Send systems and data processing people to technical training sessions from the vendor before your company installs the software.
- Don't confuse software training with general MRP education. Each is important, and neither works without the other.
- Understand the amount of time required for system installation and the advantages and disadvantages of different alternatives.
- It is critical for the vendor to provide you with a standard test sequence so you can verify that you have the right version and that the software is generating the right results.
- Your own standard test files should contain representative elements from your own data base. There is no need to run such an acceptance test using the full-sized data base; the time required is far too great for most companies.
- Never test using live data.
- A volume test, made up of a full-sized data base, should be used to check run and response times promised by the vendor and stipulated in the contract.
- Prepare to have someone map the data from the old system to the new.
- Never let systems and data processing people make changes or modifications without input from the users.
- Never do a cold turkey cutover; gradually ease into the cutover through temporary interfaces that preserve old subsystems.
- Make sure the software is as complete as possible before doing your Conference Room Pilot.

Chapter 9

Cutting the Umbilical Cord:
The Self-Sufficient MRP II Operation

We're all in this together—by ourselves.
(Lily Tomlin, comedienne)

"Diamonds are forever," or so say the advertisements. If only the same thing could be said for your relationship with the software supplier. At some time—perhaps sooner, perhaps later— you'll have to take over the maintenance, operation, and support of the software package. You'll find that making the transition to supporting the software yourself is easiest when you plan from the beginning, even prior to the actual purchase of the package.

So whether you are currently evaluating, implementing, or actually operating software for MRP II, *now* is the time to plan on ending the vendor/customer relationship. *Now* is also the time for putting in place the plan for managing and maintaining support during the transition period. And *now* is the time to develop the management checkpoints and performance measurements necessary to assure a smooth technical operation of the system.

THE END OF AN ERA

Many purchasers of packaged software bet that the vendor will support the package indefinitely. Most of them lose this bet. Over a period of years, most, if not all, vendors reduce or eliminate support services on a software package. The history of packaged MRP and MRP II software shows that even the most well-known companies will eventually reduce support on a package or drop it entirely. In some cases, vendors have even dropped more than one package.

Why do vendors stop supporting their MRP II packages? First, for a software package to be salable (note salability and usability are different), the system will probably have to incorporate most of the latest technology considered "mainstream" by professional systems and data processing people. For example, around 1974, the idea of using data base management systems like DL/I, IDMS, and TOTAL, rather than older file management software like DBOMP, became widely accepted. Consequently, between 1974 and 1978 most major mainframe software suppliers gradually eliminated their DBOMP based software and released data base oriented versions of the same software, or they dropped the DBOMP based software and released entirely new software. Vendors who didn't keep up in the past are only minor footnotes in the history of MRP II software. And without guessing what technology will provide the base for future MRP II systems, the same is likely to happen to those who don't keep up in the future.

As vendors move to incorporate new technology into their products, they become increasingly pressured to drop support on the old. Even though you may feel quite good about the results from the software you purchased 10 years ago, and have no plans to change the technology base of the system, the vendor may have entirely different plans.

Even if there are no major technological shifts, many software vendors today find themselves burdened by increasingly more complex systems. This brings us to the second reason that a vendor may eventually drop support on an MRP II package: as a piece of software evolves, it is more and more likely that the vendor will try to include features to meet the needs and wants of everyone. Besides being impractical (from a development perspective), many features will end up in the category of "reads well, works lousy." (Even more unfortunate is the fact that, in the software business, it is considerably harder to take something out of the product than it is to put it in at the beginning.) And many of the features that are added to the system won't fit the underlying architecture of the system very well, causing subsequent problems in supporting the system.

Why is this so? Simply stated, as a piece of software becomes more complex, it also becomes more difficult for the software vendor (and your own programming staff) to add new functions. The analysis and testing required to make the simplest change become quicksand on the road to progress. Consequently, the natural course of events may be for a software supplier to remove the package from the marketplace altogether and start from scratch.

Even if the vendor does not consciously drop support on the package you purchased, there are other situations that may cause the end of the vendor/customer relationship. For example, you may find, as many customers do, that the value of the support does not justify the expense. The fact of the matter is that the vendor is not accountable for making the system work on the computer—you are. By the time MRP II is up and running in the factory, most, if not all, of the major functional problems will probably have been corrected, and many of them will have been fixed by you. Since the software changes that you make aren't typically reflected in the vendor's standard version, the software supplier will be of little help in supporting the system through successive releases. In addition, if the software has been around for a few years, the number of outstanding bugs are probably at a manageable level. As a result, you may simply decide that the annual $50,000 to $100,000 maintenance fee for your mainframe software isn't buying $50,000 to $100,000 worth of benefits. In this situation, you are wise to stop paying for maintenance you don't use.

Finally, the vendor may have financial problems and be forced out of business, or into reorganization under the bankruptcy laws. In either cases, vendor support levels drop dramatically (or cease completely).

How Long Do You Have?

Some might ask, "But why not take support for as long as it lasts, and then switch to a new system?" There are three answers. First, a piece of software purchased in 1986 will probably be used in your company for eight to 20 years. There are no guarantees that the vendor will sell or support the system during that period. And although you will pay off the cost of the software in the six to 24 months following implementation, the hassle factor, confusion, and trauma caused by trying to replace the system will probably be a powerful argument for staying with the system, even if the vendor does drop support.

Second, paying for the vendor's support after the first few years is extremely expensive in real terms. The maintenance fee is eight to 15 percent of the package price. And just paying the fee doesn't entitle you to support—you must keep your version up to date with the vendor's latest release level. Consequently, you are probably paying an amount equivalent to the maintenance fee (or more) for your own people to maintain interfaces and modifications, install new releases from the vendor, test the new releases, reinstall the modifications and interfaces, and test the modifications and interfaces after reinstallation.

Last, switching software is not a trivial exercise, and is one most companies don't want to undertake under pressure. Since one of the reasons that a company might lose support is that the vendor goes out of business, a company should begin preparing as soon as it can for the transition to self-sufficiency.

Some Questions to Ask Today

As stressed above, the best time to prepare for self-sufficiency is before you buy the software. But regardless of what stage of investigation, installation, or operation you are in, you should be asking questions such as the following:

Is the software vendor financially stable? How much longer can we expect this vendor to be in this business?

How good is this vendor's track record in supporting this and other packages? Is there any demonstrated life cycle with software packages from this vendor? Where is this software package if fitted to the historical life cycle? How old is this software package? Are there known competitive pressures that could force the vendor to replace the package with a newer one sometime in the future?

What is the real value of the support services provided by the vendor?

How long would it take us to get ready to support this system if we had to?

What are the experiences of other companies that have used this software or dealt with this vendor? What about companies that have dropped support? Have they been able to use the system without major disruptions? Would they do it again?

Knowing Your Alternatives

A prudent purchaser and user of software should understand the various alternatives when faced with loss of support:

Alternative #1: Contract with a third party. Except for a few limited situations, it's unlikely this would even be possible. If a vendor goes out of the software business entirely, however, there may be some former employees who could supply temporary support, perhaps long enough for you to become self-sufficient.

Alternative #2: Buy a new software package and start all over. Not only is the process of replacing software traumatic and expensive, there are no guarantees that the new vendor won't also stop supporting the package sometime in the near future. In fact, this approach, like the first, avoids the real issue of having people in-house who are capable of supporting the system.

Alternative #3: Develop the resources to support the system internally. This is clearly the most sensible choice. I always advise my clients to plan on vendor support for two to five years, so they must do a good enough job of evaluating packages and vendors to provide two to five years of preparation time. During this time, they should be developing the internal resources necessary to support the package.

Following the initial preparation time with a package, a company should be able to rely on their own systems and data processing staff for support. This is not to say that they must be supporting the package internally at this time; rather, it means that they should be prepared to do so if they lose support or choose to sever ties with the vendor.

Factors That Affect Your Ability to Support Yourself

Many people feel uncomfortable even thinking about maintaining a software package without help from the original vendor. Yet, there are a number of instances where companies have successfully done so, for years. For example, one New Hampshire company was an early user of the IBM PICS package. Although IBM no longer supports PICS—and hasn't for a number of years—the New Hampshire company still uses it, along with many enhancements, improvements, and a modern data base management system, as the basis for its MRP II. Today, 18 years later, the company has recovered its investment in the implementation of MRP II some 20 times over, and is only now beginning to think about replacing its software.

Naturally, it does take a lot of hard work to support a system using internal resources for nearly two decades. In most cases, though, a reasonably competent systems and data processing staff can support a package functionally. For example, the Class A users of PICS (who represent a significant percentage of all Class A companies even today) have been able to develop the software necessary for functions such as firm planned orders, financial planning interfaces, and master production scheduling even though they did not exist when PICS became available.

A more difficult part of supporting a package begins when basic data processing technologies change. The introduction of new disk technologies, access methods, and data base management systems, for example, generally demands a high level of specific expertise, which you might not have in your company. On the other hand, the PICS users are once again an excellent group to look to for practical experience with this problem—and in many cases, these companies were able to take a batch oriented, DBOMP-based system and rewrite it for on-line, data base management system support.

If you need to decide whether your company can support a package internally, you should consider:

1. *Your staff's understanding of the application.* Probably the most important factor in developing internal support is your staff's understanding of MRP II and how the software package works with

respect to those concepts. Without having a thorough technical and conceptual understanding of the system, meaningful self-support will be virtually impossible.

2. *The availability of source code.* Object code only software has serious drawbacks if the vendor decides to stop supporting it. It may be possible, however, to avoid this problem in part by negotiating the proper software contract.

3. *The complexity of the software.* The more codes, features, options, and switches that are part of the system, the harder it will be to maintain.

4. *The data processing technology used to develop the software.* Your support effort will be greatly simplified if you have software written in reasonably current programming languages, and you use a current data base management system and TP monitor. In contrast, buying an MRP II system written in Assembler or using an obsolete data base management system may be a fast track to support nightmares.

MANAGING THE TRANSITION

Again, the best way to handle the transition from vendor support to internal support of the software is to plan for it from the start. By making the following preparations, a motivated systems and data processing group can probably continue to operate a software system successfully for many years into the future:

1. *Get the proper initial and on-going MRP II education.* "We have met the enemy and he is us," said Pogo. How accurately this famous conclusion reflects a systems and data processing group that is responsible for supporting an MRP II implementation but has never been part of the inside and outside MRP education process. Don't fight yourself—make sure these people are part of the education process from the start, and make sure they stay up to date as MRP II evolves.

2. *Understand the software package and its architecture*. No one will feel comfortable supporting a system unless they have a thorough understanding of its architecture, mechanics, design philosophies, and essential technical issues. Money should be budgeted to send an initial group of people to the training classes offered by the vendor. After they've returned, and before support is dropped, they need to be assigned the responsibility of designing and developing in-house training for new employees and creating refresher sessions for their own staff (for training once the relationship with the vendor has ended).

3. *Stay current with technological developments*. Your systems and DP people will not be able to support the software through successive versions of hardware, operating system release levels, data base management system release levels unless they keep abreast of such technology. Money has to be budgeted for outside seminars, classes, and other sources as a means for them to keep on top of the field.

4. *Get hands-on experience early*. Have your DP people begin making changes themselves during the implementation process. Part of getting prepared for self-sufficiency takes place during the process of bringing up the software, running test files, and building interface programs and temporary bridges. All of these exercises provide good first steps in understanding the software. Experience is the best teacher. And it's never too early to start.

SOFTWARE MODIFICATIONS: MAINTAINING SUPPORT DURING THE TRANSITION PERIOD

In general, the problem with support during the transition period is the number of modifications that have probably been made to the system. Keeping track of which programs changed and how the changes were done is an essential activity. If not carried out properly, it may make problem determination more difficult than necessary and poison the on-going relationship with the vendor, whatever that may be.

There are three ways to carry out modifications and minimize support problems. The preferable way is not to make changes to vendor-supplied code at all, but rather to write separate and independent programs that carry out the changes. In addition, rather than updating existing data elements, new data elements should be appended to existing files. For example, several companies added back scheduling logic to the original version of IBM's MAPICS package by creating separate back scheduling programs and carrying the operation start and due dates from back scheduling as new data elements in the operation detail file.

In some situations, it is impossible to do anything but change the vendor's code. Suppose, for example, that there was an error in the projected available balance calculation of MRP. If this were the case, there would be no alternative to fixing the software vendor supplied code. You would have to identify the program module, locate the line or lines that are in error, and fix them.

In this case, the best approach is generally to keep a backup of the unmodified version of the program. The backup is a point of comparison if there are problems with the modification. With this type of change, it is also incumbent upon the user to make sure every type of change has been documented. Some kind of comment should be appended to each line of the program that changed, indicating the alteration. This could be very helpful later on when someone has to troubleshoot a problem.

A third way to handle changes is to make them within user exits or subroutines. While this is a good solution in that it isolates the code, the method can only work if the software vendor has placed user exits in the right places.

However you make the changes, bear in mind that the difficulty in maintaining a piece of software through successive releases is that you have various archaeological levels of change that must be dug out and applied to each new version of the system. The more changes you make, the more excavation and insertion that has to be done. The best way to keep track of such insertions is to set up a separate library so you can quickly identify program modules that have changed, and thoroughly document every change using liberal doses of comments in the code.

Another important aspect of dealing with program changes before,

1. Put management controls in place that require justification of changes.
2. Work hard to avoid making non-essential changes.
3. Work even harder to get the essential changes done.
4. Try to make modifications through separate programs, pre- or post-processors.
5. Document code changes.
6. If necessary, develop specialized software to help identify and manage changes.
7. Understand that modifications must be applied to later releases.
8. Keep back-ups.
9. Test it *before* releasing it to the users.

Figure 9.1
Controlling software modifications

during, and after implementation is to control the impulse to make unnecessary changes. One approach for doing so is to set up a management steering committee that attempts to reduce the requested changes to a manageable number. The steering committee would be a high-level group of managers from all segments of the organization. The committee would review all requests for changes in the MRP II software, and require both a definition of the change and an economic justification of why it should be made. By including the justification phase, the steering committee can make a rational decision on which changes should be undertaken, and rank them in terms of which has the highest payback. Figure 9.1 summarizes the key points of controlling software modifications.

MANAGEMENT CHECKPOINTS AND PERFORMANCE MEASUREMENTS

A key question for systems and data processing people is "How well are we doing?" Like any other professionals, they want an objective measurement of their performance. And management, in turn, needs formal checkpoints and measurements to ensure that the important work in systems and data processing is being done effectively, to determine whether there are problems that need to be corrected, and whether the company's systems and data processing dollars are being spent wisely.

Both staff and management needs can be met through checkpoints and performance measurements like those listed in Figure 9.2 and explained below. Note that while they are not intended to be an all-encompassing list, they are a starting point for a company in need of suggestions for putting together a performance measurement program for MRP II. A company that wants to do a comprehensive job of performance measurement should take the list from Figure 9.2, add additional measurements that they feel appropriate, assess its performance, develop an action plan, and start work on improving performance. The benefit from the program is not in the measurement, but rather in developing and executing an action plan that results in improvements.

The checkpoints listed in Figure 9.2 are high-level in nature, and are somewhat subjective. Therefore, the best approach to using them is to have a number of people meet and reach a consensus. These checkpoints include:

Checkpoint #1:
Application software maintenance.

Is the money spent on software maintenance being spent wisely? Are you receiving value equal to the amount you are spending each year? What would happen if you dropped the maintenance contract? If you dropped the maintenance contract and had to start it up again, would there be any penalties?

Many companies pay $50,000 a year for software maintenance simply because no one has ever reviewed the various releases to determine whether they represent a substantial improvement. Typically, the value of support is related to:

1. The number of times there were problems that the vendor had to be consulted on.
2. The new features that were released during the year that were actually of value to your organization.

CHECKPOINT 1: Application software maintenance. Is the money spent on software maintenance being spent wisely?

CHECKPOINT 2: Application software tuning. Is the software tuned and running at optimal performance levels?

CHECKPOINT 3: Deficiency review. What system changes are essential to making MRP II work better?

CHECKPOINT 4: Backup, recovery, and restart. Do the proper procedures exist to ensure frequent backups? Do the high volume on-line systems provide for restart and recovery?

CHECKPOINT 5: Disaster planning. Is a sound disaster plan in place?

CHECKPOINT 6: Response and run times.

ACTIVITY	TARGET	PERFORMANCE
Response times		
Master schedule reporting		
Material requirements planning		
Capacity requirements planning		
Daily dispatch list		
Vendor schedule		
Input output control report		

CHECKPOINT 7: System downtime and on-line system availability

ON-LINE AVAILABILITY

Targeted number of hours per day: _____

Target start time: _____

Target end time: _____

% of time system has been up at agreed upon start time and available until target end time: _____

Downtime as percentage of targeted number of hours on-line system is planned to be available: _____

Figure 9.2
Systems and Data Processing Report Card

3. The cost of making the changes yourself.
4. Whether significant technology improvements are on the horizon.

For a rough cut at whether the support was worth the money, make a list of the number of times in the past year you've actually called the vendor and had a question, and then count the number of times the vendor could answer the question or solve the problem. Then list the specific features that were released to you during the prior year. Were any of these features of benefit to your organization, or were they bells and whistles? If you were supporting the software yourself, could you have made the changes for less money than that paid in support? Finally, is the vendor likely to offer new and upcoming technologies, for example, an interface to a relational data base management system such as IBM's DB2? If so, find out if getting the new technology requires your being tied to the support contract. Even if the support is not justified today, perhaps these technologies might justify staying with the maintenance agreement for a short time longer.

Finally, are the dollars and benefits both from support and the new features in the software sufficient to offset the amount you're paying? If they aren't and there's no significant technological improvements on the horizon, consider dropping the support.

Checkpoint #2:
Application Software Tuning.

Is the software tuned and running at an optimal performance level? In many cases, it's worthwhile having an independent hardware or software consultant, or a representative from the software vendor, come in once each year to "audit" blocking factors, buffer sizes, and various other technical elements of an MRP II system. Even if an outsider is not used, someone should be making an assessment of overall performance and what could be done to improve throughput. Usually, companies that take advantage of an outside audit find something that, when corrected, results in significant performance boosts. In most cases, such improvements in performance pay for the audit as well as the corrections several times over.

Checkpoint #3:
Annual Deficiency Reviews.

What system changes are essential to making MRP II work better? Have all the changes identified when the software was compared to *The Standard System* actually been made? What is the backlog of outstanding programming requests?

At least yearly, someone needs to be looking at the existing systems and identifying areas of improvement that will affect the bottom line. This should include an effort to identify which functions of the software were deficient and what has been done to make corrections. Part of a deficiency review entails looking at all open systems and programming requests, and determining which of these projects need to be scheduled earlier because of changing business conditions.

Checkpoint #4:
Back-up, Recovery, and Restart.

Is there a procedure for backing up files daily? Do the on-line systems provide data base logging for restart and recovery? Few companies that operate computers are without a back-up procedure, and few professionally managed data processing departments have overlooked the issues associated with restart and recovery. Nevertheless, it's still worth the effort to review these areas periodically as a way to ensure "no surprises" from systems and data processing.

A professional systems and DP department does back-ups daily, just as it has test files for system testing. In addition, a professional systems and data processing organization has a clearly defined policy on how long back-ups are kept and where the back-ups are stored. For example, a number of companies keep daily back-ups for at least a week, and take Saturday night's back-up to offsite storage. These same companies tend to have a well-defined policy and keep some back-ups as long as six months in case of catastrophic situations. Where no offsite storage is easily available, back-ups are commonly stored in a fireproof vault.

A heavily used on-line system should also have the capability of recovering from an on-line failure without having to use the back-up tapes. In some cases, restart and recovery is a function of the data base management system, rather than the application software. Sometimes a restart capability is built into the system, but the user must consciously select it when the system is generated.

Generally, when restart and recovery facilities are provided, the system can identify that a transaction has aborted in process, and then using the data base log file, back out the transaction in process and get the data base back to its status at the last so-called "quiet point." This eliminates the need to retrieve the back-up tapes and re-enter a day's worth of transactions. The only transactions that must be re-entered are those that were in process at the time of the failure.

In any high volume on-line application, if the software has no capability for restart, your programming department will probably have to create one.

Checkpoint #5:
Disaster Planning.

Is a sound disaster plan in place? No one wants to think that disasters are possible, yet they do happen every day; fires, explosions, and other tragedies can seriously damage or destroy computing facilities. Total system failures or power outages can put your processing hours or days behind. With an operating MRP II system, if the computer is down for a number of days or weeks, it may be difficult to operate the business at the same high levels of performance, and as a result there may be serious financial and customer service implications. Remember, if there were an effective manual equivalent to an MRP II system, you wouldn't need a computer in the first place.

Given your dependency on the system, you must have a contingency plan for the kinds of major disasters cited above. Part of this contingency planning is doing daily back-ups. But adequate disaster planning goes beyond back-ups and addresses the unpleasant event of hardware loss. What would you do if you lost the use of your computer?

One candidate for a very temporary replacement machine might be the local office of the hardware company that supplied you with your computer. A more likely possibility is a nearby company that has the same computer. You might be able to strike up an arrangement whereby in case of a disaster in your company, you can use the other company's computer, and vice versa. (If you're wondering what happens if there's a disaster in both companies, forget it—there will be far more serious problems to solve than what computer to use.) If you don't know of a company that has a similar configuration to your system, contact your hardware vendor. He should be able to provide a list of the nearest installations.

Finally, there are commercial outfits that are in the business of providing computer capacity in disaster situations. You may be able to locate one with reasonable rates and a plan that matches your needs.

Checkpoint #6:
Response and Run Times.

What are the goals for average response times? Are current response times within an acceptable tolerance of the goal? Are the run times by job within acceptable limits? Acceptable response times normally fall in the range of subseconds to 12 seconds. Clearly subsecond response times are ideal, but impractical for most companies. Experts say that response times above 12 seconds are not acceptable. Every company has to set an objective for reasonable response times. In my experience, if they are on the average four seconds, no one can say the system is unworkable.

Each company must also set a goal for acceptable run times for each batch job. These goals are normally set by taking into account the amount of time available to run the job, and the acceptable on-time delivery standard required by the users. If the acceptable on-time delivery goal is low, the run time can probably be longer, and there will be less work done to reduce the time required. If the on-time delivery objective is very high, however, a company will probably go to a great deal of effort to reduce the run time, or provide for checkpoint/restart capabilities.

Checkpoint #7:
System Downtime and On-line System Availability.

What is the target (number of hours per day, start time and end time) for on-line system availability? What percentage of the time is the on-line system available during the agreed upon hours? What percentage of the time is the on-line system down during the prime processing hours?

There are two basic measurements here. One is whether the on-line system is available during the agreed upon hours. If the system is available at the agreed upon start time and is taken down at the agreed upon stop time, then the system is considered available for the performance measurement. If the system comes up late or has to be taken down early, then it is considered not available for the performance measurement. Performance is determined by taking the number of available days and dividing by the total number of work days in the period.

The second measurement is the percentage of total time that the system is down. (This may require a performance monitor for accurate measurement.) The basic idea is to measure the downtime during prime hours for on-line activity. Be careful how you analyze the situation, though. One mistake that people make is to measure downtime as a percentage of total time in a week, counting third shift. This is misleading, because downtime must be based on the actual time when there is activity on the system.

PERFORMANCE MEASUREMENTS

There are a number of performance standards that your system should meet for various functions. Figure 9.3 gives some basic systems and data processing performance measurements for MRP II. These include

ON TIME DELIVERY OF:	SUGGESTED TARGET	AGREED UPON TARGET	LATEST PERFORMANCE
Sales and operations plan	100%	_____	_____
Master schedule report	99%	_____	_____
Material requirements plan	98%	_____	_____
Capacity requirements plan	98%	_____	_____
Daily dispatch list	98%	_____	_____
Vendor schedule	98%	_____	_____
Input output control report	98%	_____	_____

Figure 9.3
Performance Measurements

the name of the measurement, the recommended objective, and a tolerance if appropriate. For the most part, you'll find them self-explanatory.

SUMMARY

- Plan well in advance for the day when support for your MRP II package will cease.
- Ultimately there is no substitute for being self-sufficient.
- Your staff's understanding of the technical dimensions of the package, the state-of-the-art in new technology, and the overall principles of MRP II is a key factor in attaining self-sufficiency.
- In preparation for supporting your own package, make sure your systems and DP staff have plenty of hands-on experience working with the software, documenting their changes, and solving problems.
- It may be reasonable to drop support even though the vendor still offers it; review your maintenance contract each year and make sure you're getting your money's worth. Don't renew simply because you've done so each year in the past.

- As part of your support review, make sure that you have adequate back-up procedures in place, as well as worst-case disaster plans for the partial or total loss of your system.

- You can never do too much up front planning. Remember, the best time to make an escape plan is before you need it.

Chapter 10

Epilogue:
The Road Yet Taken

Time is a dressmaker specialising in alteration.
(Faith Baldwin, writer)

In 1975, while I worked at Ohaus Scale Corporation, we were visited by representatives of an established and well-known company that had been a pioneer in MRP. In comparing notes on MRP, we discovered that the pioneering company's MRP system did not include certain capabilities that had become standard functions within MRP. When we asked them why their software didn't include these functions, they brushed off the question saying, "Oh, those things weren't even invented when we put in MRP."

Sadly, this older, established MRP user was an example of a company in a state of "arrested development." Apparently, no one had thought it important to keep their people or their systems current with the latest thinking in the field. They had been stuck in the early sixties for nearly 15 years.

No responsible manager permits products, people, or processes to become obsolete. Why should software and systems be treated any differently from these other important resources? As MRP pioneer George Bevis concluded in the mid-1970s (he was then senior vice president at The Tennant Company), "MRP is a journey, not a destination." And he's right. Every year people learn to use systems more effectively, so the journey to manufacturing excellence is an ongoing one—even for companies that are already doing a first rate job.

Keeping your software and systems current is an important part of your continuing journey into MRP II. But as we've seen again and again, people are the most essential part of any system that works. People who are motivated to work as a team, who are armed with modern tools and the knowledge of how to use them, and who have clear management direction can truly compete "toe-to-toe" anywhere on earth.

The challenge for management for the remainder of this century is to use all the resources of the company—its people and systems, plant and products, proven processes and innovative technologies—to become world-class competitors.

The Mechanics of Manufacturing Resource Planning (MRP II)

Section 1
The Closed Loop System

The logic of the closed loop MRP system is extremely simple. It's in every cookbook. The "bill of material" says, "Turkey stuffing takes one egg, seasoning, bread crumbs, etc." The routing says, "Put the egg and the seasoning in a blender." The blender is the work center. The master schedule is Thanksgiving.

But, in manufacturing, there is a lot more volume and a lot more change. There isn't just one product. There are many. The lead times aren't as short as going to the corner store. The work centers are busy rather than waiting for work—because some of them cost a third of a million dollars or more—and it simply is not wise economically to let them sit idle and to have excess capacity. In addition, the sales department will undoubtedly change the date of Thanksgiving several times before it actually arrives! And this isn't through perversity. This is because the customers want and need some things earlier or later.

The volume of activity in manufacturing is monumentally high; something is happening all the time. And change is the norm, not the exception.

But the point is that the *logic* of MRP is very straightforward indeed. Figure A-1 shows the closed loop system.

The production plan is the *rate* of production for a product family typically expressed in units like, "We want to produce 1100 Model 30 pumps per week." The production plan is made by taking into account current inventory, deciding whether inventory needs to go up or down during the planning period, projecting the sales forecast, and determining the rate of production required to maintain, raise, or lower the inventory level. For a make-to-order product, as opposed to a make-to-stock product, the "order backlog" rather than the inventory is the starting point for the production plan.

Figure A-2 shows a typical production plan. Figure A-3 shows a business plan which is simply an extension of the production plan into dollars. The complete business plan in a manufacturing company will include research and development and other expenses not directly related to production and purchases. But the core of any business plan in a manufacturing enterprise is the production plan. With MRP II, the production plan and business plan are interdependent and, as the production plan is updated, it is extended into dollars to show it in the common denominator of business—money.

The closed loop MRP system then takes a master schedule ("What are we going to make?"), "explodes" this through the bill of material ("What does it take to make it?"), and compares

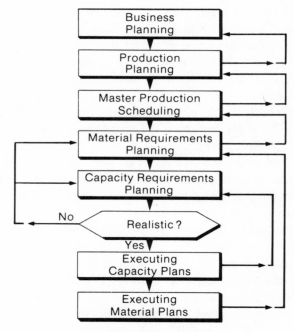

Figure A-1 MRP II

Month Ending		Sales (thousands)	Production (thousands)	Inventory (thousands)
3/31	Plan			
	Actual			60
4/30	Plan	30	35	65
	Actual	25	36	71
6/30	Plan	30	35	75
	Actual			

Figure A-2 Production Plan

this with the inventory on hand and on order ("What do we have?") to determine material requirements ("What do we have to get?").

This fundamental material requirements planning logic is shown in Figure A-4. Figure A-5 shows the bill of material. For this example, a small gasoline engine for a moped is the product being manufactured. The bill of material shown in Figure A-5 is what's known as an "indented bill of material." This simply means that the highest level items in the bill of material are shown farthest left. For example, the piston assembly components are "indented" to the right to indicate that they go into that assembly. Therefore, in this example, they are at "level 2."

A bill of material "in reverse" is called a "where-used" list. It would say, for example, that the locating pins go into the crankcase half-left, which goes into the engine.

Month Ending		Sales (thousands)	Production (thousands)	Inventory (thousands)
3/31	Plan			
	Actual			6,000
4/30	Plan	3,000	3,500	6,500
	Actual	2,500	3,600	7,100
5/31	Plan	3,000	3,500	7,000
	Actual	3,800	3,200	6,500
6/30	Plan	3,000	3,500	7,500
	Actual	3,200	3,700	7,000
12/31	Plan	3,000	3,500	10,500
	Actual			

Figure A-3 Business Plan

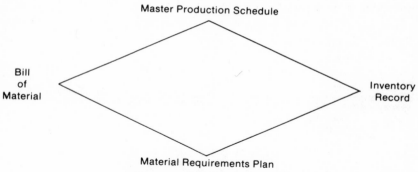

Figure A-4 MRP Logic

Part Number	
87502	Cylinder Head
94411	Crankshaft
94097	Piston Assembly
91776	Piston
84340	Wristpin
81111	Connecting Rod—Top Half
27418	Connecting Rod—Bottom Half
81743	Piston Rings Compression (2)
96652	Piston Ring Oil
20418	Bearing Halves (2)
59263	Lock Bolts (2)
43304	Crankcase Half Right
28079	Crankcase Half Left
80021	Locater Pins (2)

Figure A-5 Moped Engine Bill of Material

Master Production Schedule
Engines

	Week							
	1	2	3	4	5	6	7	8
Master Schedule	80	0	100	0	0	120	0	120
Actual Demand	40	40	30	30	30	40	40	20
Available to Promise	0	0	10	0	0	40	0	100

Figure A-6 Master Production Schedule

Figure A-6 shows a master schedule for engines. In a make-to-stock company, the master schedule would be very similar, but it would take into account the inventory on hand.

Section 2
Material Requirements Planning

Figure A-7 shows the material requirements plan for the crankcase half-left and also for the locater pin that goes into the crankcase half-left. The projected gross requirements come from the master schedule plus any service parts requirements. "Scheduled receipts" are the orders that are already in production or out with the vendors. The projected available balance takes the on-hand figure, subtracts requirements from it, and adds scheduled re-

Material Requirements Plan
Crankcase Half — Left

LEAD TIME = 4 WEEKS ORDER QUANTITY = 200		Week							
		1	2	3	4	5	6	7	8
Projected Gross Requirements		80	0	100	0	0	120	0	120
Scheduled Receipts				240					
Proj. Avail. Bal.	120	40	40	180	180	180	60	60	-60
Planned Order Release					200				

Material Requirements Plan
Locater Pin (2 Per)

LEAD TIME = 4 WEEKS ORDER QUANTITY = 500		Week							
		1	2	3	4	5	6	7	8
Projected Gross Requirements					400				400*
Scheduled Receipts									
Proj. Avail. Bal.	430	430	430	430	30	30	30	30	-370
Planned Order Release					500				

*Requirements from Another Crankcase

Figure A-7 Material Requirements Plan

ceipts to it. (In Figure A-7, the starting on-hand balance is 120 for the crankcase half-left.) This calculation projects future inventory balances to indicate when material needs to be ordered or rescheduled.

The material on hand and on order subtracted from the gross requirements yields "net requirements" (60 in week 8 for the crankcase half-left in Figure A-8). This is the amount that is actually needed to cover requirements. When the net requirements are converted to lot sizes and backed off over the lead time, they are called "planned order releases."

The "planned order releases" at one level in the product structure—in this case 200 "crankcase half-left"—become the projected gross requirements at the lower level. The 200-unit planned order release in period four for the crankcase half-left becomes a projected gross requirement of 400 locater pins in period four since there are two locater pins per crankcase half-left.

MRP — Rescheduling
Crankcase Half — Left

LEAD TIME = 4 WEEKS ORDER QUANTITY = 200		Week							
		1	2	3	4	5	6	7	8
Projected Gross Requirements		80	0	100	0	0	120	0	120
Scheduled Receipts					240				
Proj. Avail. Bal.	120	40	40	-60	180	180	60	60	-60
Planned Order Release					200				

MRP — Locater Pin (2 Per)

LEAD TIME = 4 WEEKS ORDER QUANTITY = 500		Week							
		1	2	3	4	5	6	7	8
Projected Gross Requirements					400				400*
Scheduled Receipts									
Proj. Avail. Bal.	430	430	430	430	30	30	30	30	-370
Planned Order Release					500				

*Requirements from Another Crankcase

Figure A-8 MRP—Rescheduling

Most MRP systems also include what is called "pegged requirements." This is simply a way to trace where the requirements came from. For example, the pegged requirements for the locater pins would indicate that the 400 in period four came from the crankcase half-left and that the 400 in period eight came from another product. Pegged requirements show the quantity, the time period, and the higher level item where the requirements are coming from.

Figure A-8 shows the same crankcase half as in Figure A-7. Note, however, that now the scheduled receipt is shown in period four. This means that the due date on the shop order or the purchase order is week four. An MRP system would generate a reschedule message for the planner to move the scheduled receipt from week four into week three to cover the requirements in week three.

Note, also, that the fact that the scheduled receipt for the crankcase half needs to be rescheduled does not affect the requirements for locater pins. The locater pins have already been released into production for the crankcase halves that are on order. The "requirements" for locater pins are for planned orders that have *not* been released yet.

The bill of material is the instrument for converting planned order releases at one level into projected gross requirements at a lower level. The bill of material for the crankcase half-left, for example, would show that two locater pins per crankcase half were required.

Section 3
Capacity Planning and Scheduling

Capacity planning for the manufacturing facility follows the same general logic as the material requirements planning shown in Figure A-4. Figure A-9 shows this capacity requirements planning logic. The remaining operations on released shop orders and all of the operations on planned order releases are "exploded" through the routings (like bills of material for operations) and posted against the work centers (like an inventory of capacities). The result is a capacity requirements plan in standard hours by work center showing the number of standard hours required to meet the material requirements plan. This capacity requirements plan shows the capacity that will be required to execute the master schedule, and consequently, the production plan.

It's important to note that everything in a closed loop MRP system is in "lock step." If the capacity to meet the material requirements plan can't be obtained either through a company's own manufacturing facilities, subcontracting, or purchasing material on the outside, obviously the master schedule will have to be changed. But that is the last resort. The objective is to make the master schedule happen.

Operations scheduling involves assigning individual schedule dates to the operations on a shop order using scheduling rules. Scheduling rules would typically be similar to these:

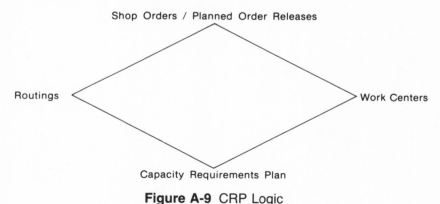

Figure A-9 CRP Logic

1. Allow two days for inspection. (This is a matter of judgment.)

2. Round the standard hours up to the nearest day.

3. Allow X days for queue time.

4. Release work to stockroom one week prior to first operation.

Scheduling with a regular calendar is extremely awkward. For example, if a job was to be completed on August 31 (see Figure A-10) and the last operation—inspection—was scheduled to take two days, the previous operation would have to be completed on August 27, not August 29 (Sunday) or August 28 (Saturday). The scheduler would have to reference the calendar continuously to avoid scheduling work on weekends, holidays, during plant vacation shutdown week, etc. Figure A-11 shows a "shop calendar" where only the working days are numbered. This allows the scheduler to do simple arithmetic like "subtract two days from day 412," thus the previous operation is to be completed on day 410.

Calendar						
AUGUST						
S	M	T	W	T	F	S
1	2	3	4	5	6	7
8	9	10	11	12	13	14
15	16	17	18	19	20	21
22	23	24	25	26	27	28
29	30	31				

Figure A-10 Calendar

Calendar						
AUGUST						
S	M	T	W	T	F	S
1	2 391	3 392	4 393	5 394	6 395	7
8	9 396	10 397	11 398	12 399	13 400	14
15	16 401	17 402	18 403	19 404	20 405	21
22	23 406	24 407	25 408	26 409	27 410	28
29	30 411	31 412				

Figure A-11   Calendar

Shop calendars are in very common use in manufacturing companies today, but they do have drawbacks. People don't relate to these calendars as easily as they do to a regular calendar. And, of course, they are awkward in dealing with customers who don't use the same shop calendar. Therefore, the shop calendar dates must, once again, be translated back to regular calendar dates. There is a simple solution to this problem with today's computers. A shop calendar can be put in the computer and the computer can do the scheduling using the shop calendar, but print the schedule dates out in regular calendar days. If a company has a shop calendar, there is no reason to discontinue using it if people are used to it. On the other hand, there is no need to introduce the shop calendar today when the computer can do the conversion.

Figure A-12 shows a shop order for the locater pin. This will be used as an example of operations scheduling and, in this example, a shop calendar *will* be used in order to make the arithmetic of scheduling clear. The due date is day 412 and that is determined, in the case of the locater pin that goes into the crank-case half-left, from the material requirements plan.

Operations scheduling works back from this need date to put scheduled finish dates on each operation using scheduling rules like those discussed above. Inspection will be allowed two days. Thus, finish turn must be completed on day 410. It is assumed that the work center file indicates that there are two shifts working in work center 1204 (two shifts at 8 hours apiece equals 16 hours), thus the 27.3 hours required for finish turn will take two days. Planned queue time in this example is assumed to be two days ahead of finish turn. Rough turn must be completed four days earlier than the finish turn must be completed, and its scheduled finish date, therefore, is day 406. The standard hours are calculated by multiplying the quantity by the time per piece and, in this case, adding in the setup time. Where machine operators do not set up their own machines, it might make sense to keep this separate.

It is important to recognize that Figure A-12 shows the information that would be in the computer. *The finish dates would not appear on the shop paperwork that was released to the factory.* The reason is that material requirements planning would be constantly reviewing the need date to see if it had changed. If, for example, the left crankcase halves are scrapped because of a problem with the castings, and the best possible date to have a new lot of castings for the crankcase halves is day 422, the master

Shop Order NN. 18447
Part No. 80021 — Locater Pin
Quant. 500   Due: 412   Release 395

Oper.	Dept.	Work Center	Desc.	Setup	Per Piece	Std. Hrs.	Finish
10	08	1322	Cut Off	.5	.010	5.5	402
20	32	1600	Rough Turn	1.5	.030	16.5	406
30	32	1204	Finish Turn	3.3	.048	27.3	410
40	11		Inspect				412

Figure A-12 Shop Order NN. 18447

schedule would be changed to indicate that. The shop order for the locater pins in the computer would be given a new finish date of 422 and operation 30 would then become 420, operation 20 would become 416, etc.

Capacity requirements will not be posted against the work centers using the routine shown in Figure A-9. A capacity plan, as shown in Figure A-13, will be the result.

This capacity plan has, of course, been cut apart to show it in the figure. It would include many more shop orders, as well as the planned order releases from MRP, in reality. The locater pins are shown here as a released shop order. (Note: there is no released shop order for locater pins in Figure A-8. It would show as a "scheduled receipt" if there were.) One of the great values of MRP is the fact that it projects "planned order releases." These planned order releases are used to:

1. Generate lower level material requirements.

2. Generate capacity requirements.

3. Determine when lower level material—both purchased and manufactured—must be rescheduled to earlier or later dates.

This ability to see capacity requirements ahead of time is especially important to good manpower planning. Seeing the capacity requirements coming rather than seeing the backlogs of

Part No.	SO No.	Qty.	Week 396-400	Week 401-405	Week 406-410	Week 411-415	Week 416-420
			Work Center	**1600**			
91762	17621	50		3.5			
80021	18447	500			16.5		
Includes Planned Orders							
Total Std. Hrs.			294	201	345	210	286

Figure A-13 Capacity Requirements Plan

work out on the factory floor enables factory supervision to do a far better job of leveling production, resulting in less overtime, and less need to hire and lay off people on a short-term basis.

Figure A-14 shows a summary of the capacity requirements over an eight-week period. In practice, this would typically be projected over a far longer period. The summary is drawn from the capacity requirements plan illustrated in Figure A-13 which would also extend much further into the future than the five weeks shown. A typical manpower plan would extend three to six months into the future and would be calculated weekly. A "facilities plan" that would be used for determining what new machine tools were needed would be calculated typically once every two to three months and extended three to four years into the future because of the lead time for procuring machine tools.

The most important information for a foreman is the average hours that he must plan to turn out. This production rate is usually calculated as a four-week average because the individual weekly hours are not particularly significant. The variations between these hours are more random than real. Figure A-13 shows one reason why this happens. The 16.5 hours for part number 80021, the locator pin, are shown in the week bracketed by days 406 to 410. Referring back to Figure A-12, it can be seen that these 16.5 hours are *actually going to be in work center 1600 Tuesday of the previous week!*

Many people have tried to develop elaborate computer load

Capacity Requirements
Summary (in Standard Hours)

Week	4-Week Total	4-Week Average	Hours	Week	4-Week Total	4-Week Average	Hours
1	294			5	286		
2	201			6	250		
3	345			7	315		
4	210	1050	263	8	257	1108	277

Figure A-14 Capacity Requirements Summary (in Standard Hours)

leveling systems because they were alarmed by the weekly variation in the apparent "load" shown in the capacity requirements plan. These variations are random. They are exaggerated by the fact that capacity plans are usually done in weekly time periods, and any foreman can attest to the fact that the hours never materialize exactly the same way they are shown on the plan. The most important thing to know is the average rate of output required so that *manpower* can be planned accordingly.

In Figure A-14, the four-week averages are 263 standard hours for the first four weeks and 277 for the second four weeks, or an average of 270 standard hours per week. Now the capacity planner must determine whether that capacity requirement can be met. The first step is to find out what the output from the work center has been over the last few weeks. This is called "demonstrated capacity." (This term was coined by David Garwood and is very useful in describing the present capacity of a work center as opposed to its potential capacity when all shifts are manned, etc.)

It is the job of the capacity planner to then determine whether or not the current capacity is sufficient. Or, what needs to be done to get the capacity to meet the plan. Or—as a last resort—to feed back information that the plan cannot be met.

If the plan cannot be met, the master schedule and, perhaps, even the production plans will have to be changed. If, for example, a company has one broach and it is the only one of its type available because it was made specifically for this company, it could well become a bottleneck. If the capacity plan indicates that more hours were required at the broach than could possibly be produced, the master schedule would have to be changed to reflect this.

Once again, however, it's important to emphasize that this is the *last resort*. The job of the capacity planner is to get the capacity that is needed to meet the plan. And that is an important point to emphasize. If there is any problem that exists in practice with capacity planning, it is the fact that people expect the computer to do the capacity planning rather than recognizing that all it can do is generate numbers that will be given to an intelligent, experienced person—the capacity planner—to use in working with other people to fix capacity problems.

Once it is agreed that the capacity requirements can be met, an output control report as shown in Figure A-15 is set up. Three weeks have passed since the one in the figure was made, and the actual standard hours produced (shown in the second line of the figure) are falling far short of the required standard hours at work center 1600. The deviation in the first week was 20 hours. In the second week, it was 50 hours—for a cumulative deviation of 70 hours. In the third week, it was 80 hours, giving a total cumulative deviation of 150 hours. This is a true *control* report with a plan and feedback to show where actual output in standard hours compares with the plan. It shows the deviation from the plan. The 150 hour deviation in week three indicates that 150 standard hours of work required to produce material to meet the master schedule has not been completed.

The amount of tolerance around the plan has to be established. If it were determined, for example, that the company could tolerate being one half week behind schedule, the tolerance in Figure A-15 would be 135 standard hours. When the deviation exceeds 135 standard hours, that would require immediate attention to increase output through overtime, adding people, etc. Whenever the planned rate in the output control report is changed, the deviation will be reset to 0.

It's a good idea to show input to a work center as well as output. That way, when a work center is behind on output because a feeding work center has not given them the work, it can be de-

Output Control
Work Center 1600
Week No. 4
(in Std. Hrs.)

Today

	Week 1	Week 2	Week 3	Week 4
Planned	270	270	270	270
Actual Std.	250	220	190	
Deviation	-20	-70	-150	

Figure A-15 Output Control

tected very quickly since the input report will show the actual input below the planned input. This is called an "input/output report."

The capacity planning and output control reports are concerned with capacity. The dispatch list shown in Figure A-16 is concerned with priority.

The dispatch list is generated daily—or as required—and goes out to the shop floor at the beginning of the day. It shows the sequence in which the jobs are to be run according to the scheduled date for the operation in that work center. The movement of jobs from work center to work center is put in to the computer so that each morning the foremen can have an up-to-date schedule that is driven by MRP. If part 80021 had been rescheduled to a new completion date of day 422 as discussed above, its priority would drop on the dispatch list because its scheduled date would now be 416. This would allow part number 44318 to be made earlier. The dispatch list gives the foremen the priority of jobs so that they can pick the proper job to start next. Since the dispatch list is driven by MRP, it tells the foremen the right sequence in which to run the jobs to do the best job of preventing predicted shortages.

Dispatch List				Day 405
Work Center No. 1600				
Shop Order No.	Part No.	Qty.	Scheduled Date	Std. Hours
17621	91762	50	401	3.5
18430	98340	500	405	19.2
18707	78212	1100	405	28.6
18447	80021	500	406	16.5
19712	44318	120	409	8.4
			Total Hours	76.2

Figure A-16 Dispatch List

Section 4
The MRP Output Reports

The figures in this chapter represent the major reports that are used in a closed loop MRP system. Referring back to Figure A-1, the functions of the production plan (Figure A-2), the master schedule (Figure A-6), the material requirements plan (Figures A-7 and A-8), and the capacity requirements plan (Figure A-13) are illustrated. The output control report (Figure A-15) is the means for monitoring output against the plan to be sure that capacity plans are being executed. The dispatch list (Figure A-16) is the report for the factory to use in executing the material plans. Vendor scheduling is the way the material requirements plans are executed with the "outside factories."

It is important to emphasize the feedback functions in a closed loop system. For example, if vendors are not going to ship on time, they must send in an anticipated delay report as soon as they recognize that they have a problem. In the past, ship dates were not valid. The typical company had many past due purchase orders with the vendor. With MRP—if it is properly managed— dates will represent real need dates, and, thus, it is important to feed back information as quickly as possible to indicate when these dates cannot be met. This, of course, is also true for the factory, where the anticipated delay report should be a regular part of their feedback to the closed loop system.

A closed loop MRP system is a fairly modern development. Many companies talked about material requirements planning for years and *did* explode bills of material on a computer. But, it was the advent of the modern computer with its great processing speeds and storage capabilities that made modern MRP practical. The ability to break requirements down into weekly, or even daily, time periods rather than showing them in monthly increments, for example, helped MRP to become a scheduling system rather than just another order launching system (even though it is superior to the order point as an ordering system). The ability to plan requirements weekly—or even daily—made MRP a practical scheduling tool. Before 1971, it would be hard to find any closed loop MRP system in existence. Master scheduling was not well understood. Capacity planning and dispatching were tried, but were usually ineffective because the priority planning wasn't valid. Computers of the day couldn't keep schedules up-to-date and the people using them didn't understand how to master schedule properly to do this. Closed loop MRP is truly a product of the computer age.

Bibliography

1. *MRP II: Unlocking America's Productivity Potential*, Oliver W. Wight, published by Oliver Wight Limited Publications, Inc. Revised Edition 1984. This book describes MRP II as the missing link in productivity, explains the new set of values and responsibilities that management will have to use to get the potential improvements in productivity by using MRP II, describes how MRP II applies in every facet of the business including marketing, finance, engineering, data processing, etc., and then tells how to be a Class A user.
2. *Production and Inventory Management in the Computer Age*, Oliver W. Wight, Van Nostrand Reinhold Co., Inc., New York, NY, 1974. This is a practical guide to production and inventory control systems. It explores priority planning, capacity planning, capacity control, priority control, and management responsibilities.
3. *Material Requirements Planning*, Joseph Orlicky, McGraw-Hill Book Company, NY, 1974. This is an excellent technical exposition of material requirements planning, and that is its basic emphasis as opposed to the entire closed loop system. This would be an excellent book for a systems designer who wanted to understand the detailed logic of a material requirements planning system.
4. *Master Production Scheduling: Principles and Practice*, William L. Berry, Thomas E. Vollman, D. Clay Whybark, American Production and Inventory Control Society, Washington, DC, 1979. This is an excellent review of current master production scheduling practice at some of the best MRP users in the country.
5. *Focus Forecasting: Computer Techniques for Inventory Control*, Bernard T. Smith, Oliver Wight Limited Publications, Inc., 1984. This is a detailed explanation of the focus forecasting system. A number of different forecasting strategies can be used with the focus forecasting system. The system tests each of these against the most

recent sales to see which works best, and then uses this strategy to forecast the immediate future.

6. *DRP: Distribution Management's Most Powerful Tool*, Andre Martin, published jointly by Prentice-Hall and Oliver Wight Limited Publications, Inc., 1983. This is a description of the way distribution requirements planning and distribution resource planning can be applied in a company with branch warehouses and distribution centers. It is particularly valuable for those companies that have manufacturing which must be integrated with a manufacturing system.

7. *APICS Dictionary*, American Production and Inventory Control Society, Washington, DC, 1980.

8. *The Executive's Guide to Successful MRP II*, Oliver W. Wight, Oliver Wight Limited Publications, Inc., 1983. This is a great "icebreaker" for the top manager who is interested in a painless introduction to MRP II. It is a result of Ollie's years of experience with manufacturing executives.

9. *MRP II: Making It Happen—The Implementers' Guide to Success with MRP II*, Thomas F. Wallace, Oliver Wight Limited Publications, Inc., 1985. This book explains the justification, implementation, and operation of MRP II. It includes detailed information on project organization and responsibilities, education, data and policies, and systems and software. Checklists are included detailing the steps necessary for Class A MRP II success.

10. *High Performance Purchasing—Manufacturing Resource Planning for the Purchasing Professional*, John E. Schorr and Thomas F. Wallace, Oliver Wight Limited Publications, Inc., 1985. This book represents a new way of life for purchasing professionals. It shows how they can become high-performance contributors to the bottom line by using the tools of manufacturing resource planning. These improvements revolve around the technique of vendor scheduling, the tasks to be done, their sequence, and provides a timetable for their completion.

11. *Just-in-Time—Surviving by Breaking Tradition*, Walter E. Goddard, Oliver Wight Limited Publications, Inc., 1986. In this book, American managers from some of the country's best-run firms tell their success stories and reveal how they made the American version of the well-known Just-in-Time approach work for them. With a "back-to-basics" approach, the Just-in-Time system puts the spotlight on people and creates an environment that acknowledges the importance of teamwork and open communication.

Appendix C

Sources for Additional Information

Preparing yourself to implement a Class A MRP II system requires careful study of a huge amount of information, far more than could be included in this or any other book. The Oliver Wight Companies can provide further assistance in getting ready, including books on the subject, live education, and reviews of commercially available software packages.

OLIVER WIGHT LIMITED PUBLICATIONS, INC.

Oliver Wight Limited Publications, Inc. was created in 1981 to publish books on MRP II, written by leading educators and consultants in the field. Titles include:

Manufacturing Resource Planning: MRP II—Unlocking America's Productivity Potential by the late Oliver W. Wight. Co-published in 1984 with Van Nostrand Reinhold.

The Executive's Guide to Successful MRP II by the late Oliver W. Wight. Co-published in 1981 with Prentice-Hall.

DRP: Distribution Resource Planning—Distribution Management's Most Powerful Tool by Andre J. Martin. Co-published with Prentice-Hall, Inc. in 1983.

Focus Forecasting: Computer Techniques for Inventory Control by Bernard T. Smith. Published in 1984.

MRP II: Making It Happen—The Implementers' Guide to Success with Manufacturing Resource Planning, by Thomas F. Wallace. Published in 1985.

For more information, or to order publications, contact:

Oliver Wight Limited Publications, Inc.
5 Oliver Wight Drive
Essex Junction, VT 05452
800-343-0625 or 802-878-8161

OLIVER WIGHT EDUCATION ASSOCIATES

OWEA is made up of a group of independent MRP II educators and consultants around the world who share a common philosophy and common goals. Classes directed towards both upper- and middle-level management are being taught in various locations around the U.S. and Canada, as well as abroad. For a detailed class brochure, listing course descriptions, instructors, costs, dates, and locations, or for the name of a recommended consultant in your area, please contact:

Oliver Wight Education Associates
P.O. Box 435
Newbury, NH 03255
800-258-3862 or 603-763-5926

OLIVER WIGHT VIDEO PRODUCTIONS, INC.

The Oliver Wight Video Library offers companies the video-based materials they need to teach the "critical mass" of their employees about the principles of MRP II. The Library is accompanied by Course Guides to assist instructors in directing the discussion sessions that supplement the information on tape. For more information on obtaining the Oliver Wight Video Library, contact:

Oliver Wight Video Productions, Inc.
5 Oliver Wight Drive
Essex Junction, VT 05452
800-343-0625 or 802-878-8161

OLIVER WIGHT SOFTWARE RESEARCH, INC.

To help you make the right choice about software in a reasonable length of time, Oliver Wight Software Research (formerly known as Manufacturing Software Systems, Inc.) offers Software Evaluations and Audits, comprehensive reviews of the capabilities of many of the most popular packages on the market today. All reviews are based on the MRP II Standard System, a research document outlining all the functions required to perform manufacturing resource planning. The Standard System is also available for use as an in-house evaluation and teaching aid. OWSR also offers a three-day course entitled, "Systems, Data Processing, and Software Selection," as well as Evaluation Consulting Support, to guide companies through the in-house evaluation process.

For more information, contact:

Oliver Wight Software Research, Inc.
5 Oliver Wight Drive
Essex Junction, VT 05452
800-343-0625 or 802-878-8161

Implementation Plan

MRP II DETAILED IMPLEMENTATION PLAN

More and more people are asking for information on the implementation and operation of MRP systems. These people are not interested in being sold on MRP. MRP systems work. The proof is available and companies are using them every day. People who understand the fundamentals and the logical simplicity of MRP are looking for a proven way to implement the system.

This detailed implementation plan is a road map to help people implement MRP systems. The implementation plan outlines the basic functional areas needed to implement MRP. These functional areas are then broken down into specific milestones. This listing of broad functional areas and specific tasks provides a very practical plan.

PEOPLE USING MRP

The implementation plan is also meant for companies using an MRP system. There are many companies which have the technical part of an MRP system in place. Yet, they are not using the system well. The implementation plan can help these companies. The jobs in improving an MRP system are the same as the jobs to implement it correctly. The only difference is that some of these jobs may have already been done. If so, they can be deleted from the plan.

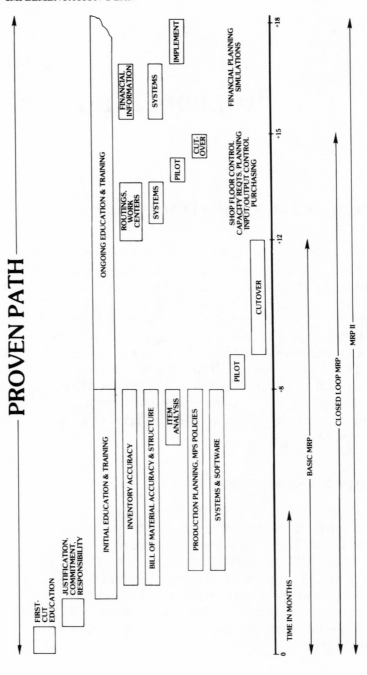

PROVEN PATH

USING THE PLAN

The implementation plan is a generalized framework applicable to nearly any company. Its two primary uses are:

1. To provide a clear statement of priorities—to separate the vital and trivial, and keep them in perspective.

2. To provide a road map for implementation.

The implementation plan is organized to constantly focus attention on the items that have the greatest impact on the potential for success. The people part of an MRP system is fully 80% of the system. The system will only work when people understand what it is, how it works, and what their responsibilities are. For this reason, the education and training are listed at the front of the implementation plan. The computer software and programming effort is not as likely to be something which prevents the success of an MRP system, and so this topic is covered later in the plan.

The other purpose is to provide a detailed schedule of events that have to be accomplished in order to implement the system. The most effective way to use the plan is to tailor the plan to each company and then use it as the agenda for management reviews of implementation progress.

PRACTICALITY

This implementation plan is not a theoretical exercise. In the six years since the first version of the plan was developed, it has been used successfully by a number of companies. Whether these companies would have been successful without the plan, I cannot say. But it does work, it is practical, and those who have used it swear by it.

TAILORING THE PLAN TO YOUR COMPANY

The implementation plan is a general framework stated in terms of departments and job titles. The departments and job titles should be replaced by the names of the people within the organization who will be responsible for the tasks.

The implementation plan also contains an approximate time frame for scheduling the tasks under each of the functional topics. The scheduled due dates for the tasks in implementation are given under the heading "DATE." These due dates were developed based on the dependence of some tasks on others. The times on the plan, +3 and +7 for example, are months relative to a starting point. A time of +3 means the task should be completed three months after the start date. The start date used in the plan is the date that formal commitment is given to the project.

The plan should be rewritten to include calendar dates in place of the scheduled completion dates in months. Columns should also be added for the scheduled start date, the actual start date, and the actual completion date. The scheduled start dates are not on the generalized plan since the size of the different tasks will vary from company to company. The actual start and actual completion dates should be included on the plan to indicate the progress or lack of it during the management reviews of implementation.

The comments column on the implementation plan is meant to give a short explanation of the phases of the plan and tasks that make up each phase. Some people choose to leave these explanations in the final version of the plan, others leave them out. In either case, additional comments on the progress of the tasks should also be included as the plan is periodically updated. These comments would indicate, for example, the results of the cycle counts, or any other information about one of the items in the plan.

A company may also have to add or delete tasks from the implementation plan to account for situations that are a part of the implementation, or work that has already been done. As an example of an item that would be deleted from the plan, a company may have already enclosed the stockrooms and may have started cycle counting. In this case, it makes no sense to count 100 parts as a starting point. As an example of an item that would have to be added to the plan, a company may have to convert to a different computer to do MRP. In this case, the conversion from one computer to the other should be included on the detailed implementation plan.

Figure C-1 is an example of the implementation plan before and after it has been tailored to a company. This example includes replacement of departments and job titles with people's names, the inclusion of calendar dates with columns for scheduling dates, and some comments on tasks that are working.

MRP DETAILED IMPLEMENTATION PLAN

TASK	RESPONSIBLE	DATE	COMMENTS
A. Measure 100 parts as a starting point.	Stockroom Mgr.	+1	This will help assess the work that needs to be done to bring the inventory records to 95%.
B. Map out limited access to the stockroom areas.	Stockroom Mgr.	+1	Lay out any stockroom changes that are necessary to insure limited access.
C. Provide the tools for limited access and transaction recording.	Top Management Stockroom Mgr. Team Leader DP Mgr.	+3	A fence, enough stockroom people, adequate space, counting scales, transaction forms, labels, skids, etc.

TASK	RESPONSIBLE	— SCHEDULED — START	DUE	— ACTUAL — START	DUE	COMMENTS
A. Measure 100 parts as a starting point.	R. Ferris	6/20/80	6/27/80	6/20/80	6/24/80	Results indicate that the inventory accuracy is 63%.
B. Map out limited access to the stockroom areas.	R. Ferris K. Miller	6/1/80	7/1/80	6/5/80		Lay out any stockroom changes that are necessary to insure limited access. Main and spare parts stockrooms to be enclosed and third stockroom to be consolidated into the existing stockrooms.
C. Provide the tools for limited access and transaction recording.	D. Roser R. Ferris K. Miller H. Arner	7/15/80	9/1/80			A fence, enough stockroom people, adequate space, counting scales, transaction forms, labels, skids, etc.

Figure C-1

MRP DETAILED IMPLEMENTATION PLAN

TASK	RESPONSIBLE	DATE	COMMENTS
1. First-cut education.	Top Management P&IC Shop Management	−1	What is MRP and how does it work? Why should we, as a company, commit to it? The courses should be the equivalent of the following courses offered by The Oliver Wight Companies P.O. Box 435 Newbury, New Hampshire 03255 (800) 258-3862 or (603) 763-5926
	Top Management P&IC Shop Management		MRP II: Manufacturing Resource Planning For Top Management MRP II: Manufacturing Resource Planning - 5 Day
2. Justification, commitment, and assignment of responsibility. A. Prepare justification.	Top Management P&IC P&IC Shop Management	0	Formal commitment to the project.
		0	Cost/Benefit.
B. Commit to the project.	Top Management	0	
C. Set up implementation team and team leader.	Top Management	0	Implementation team leader is full-time. His responsibility is to make the MRP system work by coordinating and managing the project.
D. Schedule periodic management project reviews.	Top Management	0	Approximately every month. To include all those responsible for parts of the project currently active.
E. Schedule periodic visits from a consultant with experience in implementing successful MRP systems.	Top Management	0	The consultant should have successfully implemented a system or worked with successful systems. Schedule visits from once a month to once every three months.

MRP DETAILED IMPLEMENTATION PLAN

TASK	RESPONSIBLE	DATE	COMMENTS
3. Detailed education and training.	Team Leader	0+8	This phase of the plan is aimed at the people part of the system.
			The objective of this part of the plan is to give the people operating the system an understanding of the system and the means to use it effectively. Education and training must translate the general principles of MRP into the specifics of operation at the company.
			The plan separates education and training. Education is the broad-based understanding of MRP which is essential. Training is the detailed knowledge of reports, forms, etc.
			The education and training are structured in levels. People in the company attend outside courses. These people then serve as teachers and train their own people.
A. Outside courses for people who will be teachers at the in-house courses.	Team Leader	+1+3	The courses should be the equivalent of the following courses offered by The Oliver Wight Companies P. O. Box 435 Newbury, New Hampshire 03255 (800) 258-3862 or (603) 763-5926
	Steering Committee Chairman		MRP II: Manufacturing Resource Planning—5-Day
	P&IC Mgr.		MRP II: Successful Implementation
	Purch. Mgr.		MRP II: Successful Implementation
	Plant Supt.		MRP II: Manufacturing Resource Planning—5-Day
	Stockroom Mgr.		MRP II: Manufacturing Resource Planning—5-Day
	Engr. Mgr.		MRP II: Manufacturing Resource Planning—5-Day
			MRP II: Manufacturing Resource Planning—5-Day
			MRP II: Manufacturing Resource Planning For Top Management
	Sales/Mktg. Mgr.		MRP II: Manufacturing Resource Planning For Top Management
	DP Mgr.		MRP II: Manufacturing Resource Planning—5-Day

MRP DETAILED IMPLEMENTATION PLAN

TASK	RESPONSIBLE	DATE	COMMENTS
B. Purchase or lease the MRP video courses for in-house education.	Team Leader	+1	These video courses will serve as the framework for all the educational courses in the following educational plan. The current library consists of 53 video tapes, approximately 33 hours of video taped education on MRP. The MRP video library is available through: The Oliver Wight Companies 5 Oliver Wight Drive Essex Junction, Vermont 05452 (802) 878-8161 or (800) 343-0625
C. Teachers course. Video education.	Team Leader	+1½	The team leader and all teachers go through the video courses to translate the general principles of MRP into the specifics of operation at the company. *Attendees:* All teachers. *Length:* Approx. 80 hrs.
D. Top Management Course. Video education.	Team Leader	+2+8	*Attendees:* Pres., all VPs, Plant Superintendent, others as appropriate. *Length:* Approx. 40 hrs.
E. Production and inventory control. Video education.	P&IC Mgr.	+2+8	*Attendees:* All people in P&IC. *Length:* Approx. 80 hrs.
Outside workshop	Master Scheduler	+3	Outside master scheduling workshop for one or more master schedulers. The workshop should be the equivalent of the one offered by The Oliver Wight Companies.

MRP DETAILED IMPLEMENTATION PLAN

TASK	RESPONSIBLE	DATE	COMMENTS
In-house training.	P&IC Mgr.	+7+8	*Attendees:* All people in P&IC. *Coverage:* All forms, reports, and documents that will be used by the people in P&IC. This includes a dry run of the system, sometimes called a "conference room pilot," to gain experience in using the reports and transactions.
F. Purchasing. Video education.	Purch. Mgr.	+2+8	*Attendees:* All people in purchasing. *Length:* Approx. 45 hrs.
Outside workshop.	Purch. Mgr. Buyers	+5	Outside purchasing workshop for one or more buyers. The workshop should be the equivalent of the one offered by The Oliver Wight Companies.
In-house training.	Purch. Mgr.	+7+8	*Attendees:* All people in purchasing. *Coverage:* All forms, reports, and documents that will be used by the people in purchasing. This includes a dry run of the system, sometimes called a "conference room pilot," to gain experience in using the reports and transactions.
G. Shop foreman. Video education.	VP Mfg. Plant Supt.	+2+8	*Attendees:* All shop foremen. *Length:* Approx. 40-45 hrs.
Outside workshop.	Shop Foreman	+5	Outside shop floor control and capacity requirements planning workshop. The workshop would be the equivalent of the one offered by The Oliver Wight Companies.
In-house training.	Plant Supt.	+7+8	*Attendees:* All shop foremen. *Coverage:* All forms, reports, and documents that will be used by the shop people. This includes a dry run using the documents.

MRP DETAILED IMPLEMENTATION PLAN

TASK	RESPONSIBLE	DATE	COMMENTS
H. Stockroom people. Video education.	Stockroom Mgr.	+2+4	*Attendees:* Anyone who will be making inventory transactions. *Length:* Approx. 15 hrs.
Outside workshop.	Stockroom Mgr.	+3	Outside inventory accuracy workshop for one or more stockroom managers. The workshop should be the equivalent of the one offered by The Oliver Wight Companies.
In-house training.	Stockroom Mgr.	+3	*Attendees:* Anyone who will be making inventory transactions. *Coverage;* All forms, reports, and documents that will be used in the inventory transaction system.
I. Sales and marketing. Video education.	Sales/Mktg. Mgr.	+3+8	*Attendees:* All sales and marketing people. This course is usually divided into two courses. One for those people in-house and one for those in district sales offices. *Length:* Approx. 25–30 hrs.
In-house training.	Sales/Mktg. Leader	+8	*Attendees:* All in-house sales and marketing people. *Coverage:* All forms, reports, and documents used in master scheduling and forecasting applicable to the sales and marketing people.

MRP DETAILED IMPLEMENTATION PLAN

TASK	RESPONSIBLE	DATE	COMMENTS
J. Engineering. Video education.	Engr. Mgr.	+2+8	*Attendees:* Anyone who will be working with bills of material or routings. *Length:* Approx. 30—40 hrs.
Outside workshop.	Engr. Mgr.	+3	Outside bill of material structuring workshop for the engineering manager and several of the engineers who will be structuring bills of material. The bill of material workshop should be the equivalent of the workshop offered by the Oliver Wight Companies.
In-house training.	Engr. Mgr.	+5	*Attendees:* Anyone who will be working with bills of material or routings. *Coverage:* All forms, reports, and documents that will be used to maintain bills of material and routings.
K. Data processing. Video education.	DP Mgr.	+2+8	*Attendees:* Anyone who will be working with the MRP programs or files. *Length:* Approx. 55 hrs.
L. Finance. Video education.	Mgr. Finance/ Accounting	+2+8	*Attendees:* All people in finance. *Length:* Approx. 35 hrs.
Outside workshop.	Mgr. Finance/ Accounting	+2+8	Outside finance and accounting workshop for one or more managers of finance and/or accounting. The workshop should be the equivalent of the one offered by The Oliver Wight Companies.
M. Lead men and setup men.	Shop Foremen	+2+8	*Attendees:* All setup or lead men. *Length:* Approx. 20 hrs.

MRP DETAILED IMPLEMENTATION PLAN

TASK	RESPONSIBLE	DATE	COMMENTS
N. Distribution center managers. Video education.	Distribution Mgr.	+2+8	*Attendees:* All distribution center or branch warehouse managers. *Length:* Approx. 20 hrs.
Outside workshop.	Distribution Mgr. DC Mgrs. Master Scheduler P&IC Mgr.	+3	Outside distribution resource planning workshop for the manager of distribution, one or more distribution center or branch warehouse managers, one or more master schedulers, P&IC manager. The workshop should be the equivalent of the one offered by The Oliver Wight Companies.
O. Distribution center employees. Video education.	DC Mgrs.	+3+8	*Attendees:* All distribution center employees. *Length:* Approx. 15 hrs.
P. Introduction to all direct labor employees.	VP Mfg. Plant Supt.	+3+8	*Attendees:* All direct labor employees. *Length:* Approx. 2 hrs.
Q. Anyone else affected by the system and not covered in the courses above.	Team Leader	+8	*Attendees:* As required. *Length:* As required.
4. Inventory accuracy.	Stockroom Mgr.	+8	This phase of the plan is aimed at bringing the inventory accuracy to 95% of the items within the counting error. This must be accomplished before the pilot program can be started. This includes distribution centers or branch warehouses.
A. Measure 100 parts as a starting point.	Stockroom Mgr.	+1	This will help assess the work that needs to be done to bring the inventory records to 95%.
B. Map out limited access to the stockroom areas.	Stockroom Mgr.	+1	Lay out any stockroom changes that are necessary to insure limited access.

MRP DETAILED IMPLEMENTATION PLAN

TASK	RESPONSIBLE	DATE	COMMENTS
C. Provide the tools for limited access and transaction recording.	Top Management Stockroom Mgr. Team Leader DP Mgr.	+3	A fence, enough stockroom people, adequate space, counting scales, transaction forms, labels, skids, etc.
D. Assign responsibility for the inventory accuracy.	Top Management	+3	The inventory manager and his people are now responsible for the inventory accuracy. Change job descriptions where necessary.
E. Start counting a control group of 100 parts.	Stockroom Mgr.	+3	Control group parts are counted once every ten days. Any inventory errors are investigated to find the cause of the error.
F. Each ten days a report is published showing the results of the control group.	Stockroom Mgr.	+3 on	The report should show the history of the inventory accuracy and the cause of the errors.
G. Start cycle counting all inventory items.	Stockroom Mgr.	+5 on	All parts are counted periodically. A simple method would be to count A and B items twice a year, and the C items once a year.
H. Bring the inventory accuracy to 95% of the parts within counting error.	Stockroom Mgr.	+8	As measured by the results of cycle counting the items in inventory, and not based only on the control group items.
5. Bill of material accuracy.	Engr. Mgr. P&IC Mgr.	+8	This phase of the plan is aimed at bringing bill of material accuracy to 98%. The tasks in this phase must be completed before the pilot program can begin. Both design and production engineering should participate in structuring the bills of material.

MRP DETAILED IMPLEMENTATION PLAN

TASK	RESPONSIBLE	DATE	COMMENTS
A. Measure 100 bills of material as a starting point.	Engineering	+3	This will help assess the work that needs to be done to eliminate errors from the bills of material.
B. Decide and assign responsibility for the accuracy of bills of material.	Top Management	+3	This may involve centralizing some responsibilities and setting up procedures to control the flow of documents if these are not already present.
C. Verify the bills of material for correct part numbers and quantities per assembly.	Engineering	+8	This requires either a line-by-line audit or an exception system, like stockroom pulls, to point out bill of material errors. Either method must highlight and correct any errors in component part numbers or quantities per assembly.
D. Verify the bills of material to show the correct structure of the product.	Engineering	+8	This requires restructuring the bills where necessary to show: 1. The way material moves on the shop floor. 2. Raw materials on the bills of material. 3. Modules or self-consumed assemblies where needed.
E. Decide on and implement bill of material policies.	Top Management Engineering P&IC	+5	Policies: 1. Engineering change procedure. 2. Documenting new or special products.
6. Item analysis.	P&IC Mgr.	+8	This phase of the plan covers the verification or assignment of the ordering rules.
A. Measure 100 items as a starting point.	P&IC Purchasing Team Leader	+1	The parts are checked for correct lead times, ordering quantities, and safety stock (if applicable). This measurement will help assess the work that needs to be done.

MRP DETAILED IMPLEMENTATION PLAN

TASK	RESPONSIBLE	DATE	COMMENTS
B. Agree upon and assign responsibility for the ordering rules.	P&IC Purchasing	+2	Responsibilities depend on how purchasing fits into the organization and whether or not the planner/buyer concept is used.
C. Verify or establish ordering policies.	P&IC Purchasing	+8	Decide between fixed order policy or lot-for-lot ordering. Dynamic order policies like part period balancing are not recommended.
D. Verify or establish order quantities and order modifiers.	P&IC Purchasing	+8	Assign order quantities for fixed order policy items. Modifiers should be assigned where they are appropriate.
E. Verify or establish lead times.	P&IC Purchasing	+8	*Manufactured parts:* 1. Use simple scheduling rules. 2. Be consistent. *Purchased parts:* 1. Use current lead times.
F. Verify or establish safety stock levels.	P&IC Purchasing	+8	*Independent demand items:* 1. Consistent with the master schedule policy. *Dependent demand items:* 1. In special circumstances.
7. Master production schedule preparation.	Top Management Marketing P&IC Shop Management	+8	This phase of the plan covers the work required to set up a working master production schedule. Must include resource requirements planning.
A. Develop a production planning function.	Top Management Marketing P&IC Shop Management	+6	Production planning is basic strategic planning to develop a statement of production which is in families of products and by months.

MRP DETAILED IMPLEMENTATION PLAN

TASK	RESPONSIBLE	DATE	COMMENTS
B. Develop a master scheduling function.	P&IC	+6	Master scheduling takes the production plan and translates it into a specific statement of production. The master schedule is a statement of production in specific item numbers and by weeks.
C. Develop a master schedule policy.	Top Management Marketing P&IC Shop Management	+6	The master schedule policy should cover the following points for both production planning and master scheduling: 1. Procedure for changing the production plan or master production schedule. This procedure should include who can request a change, how the proposed change is investigated, and who should approve it before it is implemented. 2. Periodic reviews of the forecast and actual sales, also the master schedule and the actual production. The purpose of these reviews is to determine whether or not the production plan or master production schedule should be changed.
D. Begin operating the production plan and master production schedule.	Top Management Marketing P&IC Shop Management	+8	The first production plan and master production schedule are developed.

MRP DETAILED IMPLEMENTATION PLAN

TASK	RESPONSIBLE	DATE	COMMENTS
8. Systems work and software selection.	DP Mgr.	+8	This phase of the plan outlines the work that needs to be done in selecting software and accomplishing the systems work and programming for the MRP system.
A. Review and select software to be used.	Data Processing P&IC Shop Management	+2	Software should be evaluated using the software evaluations from: The Oliver Wight Companies 5 Oliver Wight Drive Essex Junction, Vermont 05452 (802) 878-8161 or (800) 343-0625
B. Systems work, programming, and testing of inventory transactions.	Data Processing	+5	Issues, receipts, cycle counting.
C. Systems work, programming, and testing of bills of material.	Data Processing	+6	Normal bill of material functions.
D. Systems work, programming, and testing of scheduled receipts.	Data Processing	+6½	Scheduling receipts: 1. Manufacturing orders. 2. Purchase orders. 3. Distribution orders.
E. Systems work, programming, and testing of the MRP logic.	Data Processing	+8	Any modifications that need to be made.
F. Systems work, programming, and testing of the master schedule system.	Data Processing	+8	Master scheduling and production planning support.
G. Agree on time schedules and cutoff times.	Data Processing	+6	Times for reports, transactions and cutoff times for transactions to the system.

MRP DETAILED IMPLEMENTATION PLAN

TASK	RESPONSIBLE	DATE	COMMENTS
9. Pre-installation tasks.	P&IC Mgr. Team Leader	+8	This phase of the plan covers the tasks that immediately precede the pilot program. Must include some form of shop dispatching.
A. Set up planner structure and part responsibilities.	P&IC	+8	Which planners are responsible for which groups of parts? Decide among vertical or horizontal responsibility: 1. Vertical product line-oriented. 2. Horizontal department-oriented.
B. Set up procedures for handling both top down and bottom up closed loop planning.	P&IC Shop Foremen Purchasing	+8	Specific procedures for rescheduling, order release, and feedback of anticipated delays.
C. Physical cleanup.	P&IC Shop Foremen Purchasing	+8	Physical cleanup of the shop floor to insure that each open order has the required component parts, and that all parts on the floor are on an open order. Parts not covered by a shop order should be returned to the stockroom. All manufacturing orders and purchase orders should be verified.
10. Pilot program.	Everyone involved so far	+8+9	This is the pilot program. It is a trial run of the system on one or a group of product lines that total several hundred part numbers. The purpose is to verify that the system is giving correct information.
A. Monitor the critical measurements.	Team Leader	+8+9	Verify that the system is providing correct information and that people are comfortable using the system.

MRP DETAILED IMPLEMENTATION PLAN

TASK	RESPONSIBLE	DATE	COMMENTS
11. Cutover.	Everyone involved so far.	$+9+12$	This phase of the plan outlines the sequence that is used to move from the pilot program to full implementation on all product lines.
A. Group the remaining product lines into three or four divisions.	P&IC	$+9$	Divisions should contain product lines that are similar or share common parts.
B. Bring each division onto MRP, one division at a time.	P&IC	$+9+12$	As each division is put onto MRP, set up planner coverage so the product lines involved get intense planner coverage until they are quieted down.

END OF FIRST MAJOR SECTION IN IMPLEMENTATION

TASK	RESPONSIBLE	DATE	COMMENTS
12. Training for shop floor control, capacity requirements planning, input/output control, and purchasing.	Shop Management	$+15$	This phase of the plan outlines the training for shop floor control, capacity requirements planning and purchasing. This training has the same objectives and the same basic course outline as the MRP training covered previously.
A. Shop Foremen. In-house training.	Plant Supt.	$+15$	*Attendees:* All shop foremen. *Coverage:* All forms, reports, and documents that will be used in the shop floor control and capacity requirements planning systems.
B. Planners. In-house training.	P&IC Mgr.	$+15$	*Attendees:* All planners that will be working with the shop people. *Coverage:* All forms, reports, and documents that will be used in the shop floor control and capacity requirements planning systems.

MRP DETAILED IMPLEMENTATION PLAN

TASK	RESPONSIBLE	DATE	COMMENTS
C. Shop dispatchers. In-house training.	Shop Foremen	+15	*Attendees:* All shop dispatchers. *Coverage:* All forms, reports and documents that will be used in the shop floor control and capacity requirements planning systems.
D. Purchasing. In-house training.	Purch. Mgr.	+15	*Attendees:* All purchasing people. *Coverage:* All forms, reports and documents that will be used in vendor follow-up and vendor negotiation.
13. Routing accuracy.	Shop Foremen Prod. Engr.	+15	This phase of the plan outlines the work that needs to be done to get routing accuracy to 95%.
A. Measure 100 routings as a starting point.	Shop Foremen Prod. Engr.	+10	This will help assess the work that needs to be done to eliminate errors from the routings.
B. Decide on and assign responsibility for the accuracy of the routings.	Top Management	+11	This may involve centralizing some responsibilities or defining areas of responsibilities if these do not already exist.
C. Verify that the routings show the operations correctly.	Shop Foremen Prod. Engr.	+15	This requires either a line-by-line audit of the routing or an exception system to point out routing errors. Either method must highlight and correct the errors in the routings. The routings should be verified for the following: 1. The correct operations and work centers. 2. The correct operation sequence. 3. A reasonable standard that can be used in scheduling.

MRP DETAILED IMPLEMENTATION PLAN

TASK		RESPONSIBLE	DATE	COMMENTS
14.	Work center identification.	Shop Foremen Prod. Engr.	+15	This phase of the plan outlines the simple steps that are required to define and classify the work centers.
	A. Identify work centers.	Shop Foremen Prod. Engr.	+15	Decide which machines or groups of machines will be called work centers. In some cases a single machine will be a work center. In others, a group of similar machines will be a work center.
15.	Systems work.	DP Mgr.	+15	This phase of the plan outlines the systems work and programming that must be done for shop floor control and capacity requirements planning.
	A. Systems work, programming, and testing of shop floor control.	Data Processing	+15	Shop floor control functions.
	B. Systems work, programming, and testing of capacity requirements planning.	Data Processing	+15	Capacity requirements planning functions.
	C. Systems work, programming, and testing of input/output control.	Data Processing	+15	Input/output control report.
	D. Systems work, programming, and testing for purchasing.	Data Processing	+15	Vendor follow-up and vendor negotiation reports.

MRP DETAILED IMPLEMENTATION PLAN

TASK	RESPONSIBLE	DATE	COMMENTS
16. Implementation of shop floor control.	Shop Foremen P&IC	+15+16	The implementation of shop floor control uses a pilot program since new transactions and disciplines are being used on the shop floor.
A. Implement shop floor control on a pilot group of parts.	Shop Foremen P&IC	+15	The pilot should be large enough to provide one hundred or so shop orders. It is also helpful to use a product line that will create shop orders under shop floor control in all departments.
B. Implement shop floor control on the remaining items.	Shop Foremen P&IC	+15½	Cut over remaining items.
17. Implement capacity requirements planning, input/output control, and purchasing.	Shop Foremen P&IC Purch. Mgr.	+16	This is a simple implementation. Capacity requirements planning, input/output control, and purchasing negotiation reports are simply stated.

END OF SECOND MAJOR SECTION IN IMPLEMENTATION

MRP DETAILED IMPLEMENTATION PLAN

TASK	RESPONSIBLE	DATE	COMMENTS
18. Training for financial planning and simulation.	Mgr. Finance/ Accounting, P&IC Mgr.	+18	This phase of the plan outlines the training for financial planning and simulations. This training has the same objectives and the same basic course outline as the MRP training covered previously.
A. Finance and accounting. In-house training.	Mgr. Finance/ Accounting	+18	Attendees: People in finance and accounting. Coverage: All forms, reports, and documents that will be used.
B. Production and inventory control. In-house training.	P&IC Mgr.	+18	Attendees: People in P&IC. Coverage: Differences between simulations and normal operation of the system.
19. Develop financial planning numbers.	Mgr. Finance/ Accounting	+18	These numbers are used to do inventory projections, cash flow projections, and fixed overhead allocations. Numbers include: 1. Cost by item. 2. Labor costs. 3. Machinery operating costs. 4. Fixed overhead allocations by work center, group of work centers, or departments.

MRP DETAILED IMPLEMENTATION PLAN

TASK	RESPONSIBLE	DATE	COMMENTS
20. **Implement financial planning and simulations.**	Mgr. Finance/ Accounting P&IC Mgr.	+18	No pilot is needed. Begin running the programs and verify the numbers before using for decisions. Types of simulations available include: 1. Changed master production schedule: A. Material impact. B. Capacity impact. C. Financial impact. D. Marketing impact. 2. Make/Buy simulations. 3. Different forecast—same MPS. 4. Sales promotions—same or different MPS. 5. New product introductions.

Darryl Landvater
The Oliver Wight Companies
5 Oliver Wight Drive
Essex Junction, Vermont 05452
(802) 878-8161 or (800) 343-0625

Vendor List

A complete listing of MRP II software vendors is available from Oliver Wight Software Research, Inc. An up-to-date copy can be obtained by contacting:

Oliver Wight Software Research, Inc.
5 Oliver Wight Drive
Essex Junction, VT 05452
800-343-0625 or 802-878-8161

Non-Disclosure Agreement

This agreement is entered into this _____ day of _____, 19____, between (vendor name), a corporation organized and existing under the laws of the State of _____and having its principal place of business at _____, and (name of company requesting documentation), a corporation organized and existing under the laws of the State of _____, with its principal place of business located at _____

_____.

WITNESSETH:

WHEREAS, (name of company requesting documentation) desires to review certain written documentation which supports the (package name) computer software system and thereby evaluate said software system; and

WHEREAS, in order to conduct such review and evaluation, it is necessary for (vendor name) to disclose confidential written documentation to (name of company requesting information); and

WHEREAS, (vendor name) desires to protect the confidentiality of the written documentation to be disclosed to (name of company requesting documentation);

NOW, THEREFORE, in consideration of the mutual covenants set forth hereinafter, the parties agree as follows:

1. *Documentation to be disclosed.* (Vendor name) shall deliver and disclose to (name of company requesting documentation) one copy of the following confidential written documentation, to be used by (name of company requesting documentation) for the purpose set forth in Section 2 hereof:
   (names and #s of Manuals)
   (hereinafter collectively referred to as "Documentation").
2. *Purpose of Disclosure.* (Vendor name) disclosure of the Documentation to (name of company requesting documentation) is for the sole purpose of enabling (name of company requesting documentation) to conduct a review of the Documentation and thereby evaluate the (package name) computer software system. The Documentation delivered and disclosed by (vendor name) to (name of company requesting documentation) shall not be used for any purpose other than that stated in this Agreement; in particular, no license is granted, directly or indirectly, under any patent, copyright or any other form of proprietary rights now held by, or which may be obtained by, or which is licensed by, (vendor name).
3. *Proprietary Protection.* (Name of company requesting documentation) agrees to keep secret and confidential the Documentation and any further information relating thereto, disclosed by (vendor name) to (name of company requesting documentation). Further, (name of company requesting documentation) agrees that it will not reproduce or copy, in any manner, the Documentation delivered to it in connection with this Agreement, without the written consent of (vendor name). In order to further protect the confidentiality of the Documentation, (name of company requesting documentation) agrees that the Documentation shall be disclosed and made available only to those employees of (name of company requesting documentation) who agree to receive the Documentation under the conditions set forth herein and who require such documentation to assist (name of company requesting documentation) in evaluating the (package name) software system.
   (Name of company requesting documentation) shall not be required to keep confidential any information which it is able to prove:
   (i) Is within, or later falls within the public domain without breach of

this Agreement by (name of company requesting documentation);

(ii) Is known to (name of company requesting documentation) prior to
any disclosure by (vendor name);

(iii) Is or becomes available to (name of company requesting documentation) from a source other than (vendor name) without restric-
tion on disclosure.

In addition, (name of company requesting documentation) agrees to
use the same degree of care as it uses to prevent the disclosure of its
own confidential information, together with any additional safeguards
required for confidentiality as set forth in this Agreement.

4. *Disclosure of Evaluation Results.* (Name of company requesting
documentation) agrees that it shall not disclose the results of its review and evaluation to any other firm, person or group, other than
(vendor name).

(Vendor name) agrees that (company requesting documentation) may
disclose that it conducted a review and evaluation of (package name).

5. *Terms of Agreement.* This agreement shall remain in effect until such
time as (vendor name) makes a written request for the return or de-
struction of the Documentation and all other documentation later delivered to (name of company requesting documentation) for review.
Upon receipt of such written request, (name of company requesting
documentation) shall return or destroy all documentation relating to
the (package name) computer software system and this agreement
shall terminate; provided, however, that the terms of Section 3, Proprietary Protection, and 4, Disclosure of Evaluation Results, shall
survive the term of this Agreement.

6. *General Terms.*

6.1 Assignment. Neither party hereto may assign or transfer its rights
or obligations under this Agreement without the prior written
consent of the other party.

6.2 Waiver. No waiver by either party of any default on the part of
either party hereto, or of any right or remedy incident thereto,
shall constitute a continuing waiver of any other default, or right
or remedy hereunder.

6.3 Construction. This agreement shall be construed and enforced
according to the internal laws of the State of _____.

6.4 Amendment. No modification, amendment, waiver, or alteration
of or to this Agreement shall be binding on the parties hereto

unless made in writing and signed by an authorized representative of each.

6.5 Entire Agreement. Each party hereto acknowledges that it has read this agreement, has consulted legal counsel with respect hereto, understands the Agreement, and agrees to be bound by its terms and conditions and further agrees that it is the complete and exclusive statement of this Agreement between them.

IN WITNESS THEREOF, the parties hereto have caused this Agreement to be executed by their duly authorized representatives, said Agreement to be effective on the date first above written.

(Name of company   (Vendor name)
requesting documentation)

By: _____   By: _____

Name: _____   Name: _____

Title: _____   Title: _____

Date: _____   Date: _____

Glossary

Many of the terms found in this glossary have been drawn or adapted from the *APICS Dictionary,* Thomas F. Wallace, Editor. Reprinted with permission, American Production & Inventory Control Society, Inc., *APICS Dictionary, Fifth Edition,* 1984.

ABC CLASSIFICATION   Classification of the items in an inventory in decreasing order of annual dollar volume or other criteria. This array is then split into three classes, called A, B, and C. Class A contains the items with the highest annual dollar volume and receives the most attention. The medium Class B receives less attention, and Class C, which contains the low-dollar volume items, is controlled routinely. The ABC principle is that effort saved through relaxed controls on low-value items will be applied to reduce inventories of high-value items.

ACTION MESSAGE   An output of an MRP II system that identifies the need for and the type of action to be taken to correct a current or a potential problem. Examples of action messages are "Release Order," "Reschedule Out," "Cancel," etc.

ALLOCATION   In an MRP II system, an allocated item is one for which a picking order has been released to the stockroom but not yet sent out of the stockroom. It is an "uncashed" stock-room requisition.

ANTICIPATED DELAY REPORT   A report, normally issued by both manfacturing and purchasing to the material planning function, regarding jobs or purchase orders which will not be completed on time, why not, and when they will be completed. This is an essential ingredient of a closed loop system. Except perhaps in very large companies, the anticipated delay report is manually prepared.

AUTOMATIC RESCHEDULING   Allowing the computer to automatically change due dates on scheduled receipts when it detects that due dates and required dates are out of phase. Automatic rescheduling is not recommended.

AVAILABLE TO PROMISE   The uncommitted portion of a company's inventory or planned production. This figure is frequently calculated from the master production schedule and is maintained as a tool for order promising.

BACKFLUSH   The deduction from inventory of the component parts used in an assembly or subassembly by exploding the bill of materials by the production count of assemblies produced. *See* Post-deduct inventory transaction processing.

BACKLOG   All of the customer orders booked, i.e., received but not yet shipped. Sometimes referred to as "open orders" or the "order board."

BACK SCHEDULING   A technique for calculating operation start and due dates. The schedule is computed starting with the due date for the order and working backward to determine the required completion dates for each operation.

BILL OF MATERIAL   A listing of all the subassemblies, intermediates, parts and raw materials, etc. that go into a parent item, showing the quantity of each component required. May also be called "formula," "recipe," or "ingredients list" in certain industries.

BUCKETED SYSTEM   An MRP, DRP or other time-phased system in which all time-phased data are accumulated into time periods or "buckets." If the period of accumulation would be one week, then the system would be said to have weekly buckets.

BUCKETLESS SYSTEM   An MRP II, DRP or other time-phased system in which all time-phased data are processed, stored and displayed using dated records rather than defined time periods or "buckets."

BUSINESS PLAN   A statement of income projections, costs and profits usually accompanied by budgets and a projected balance sheet as well as a cash flow (source and application of funds) statement. It is usually stated in terms of dollars only. The business plan and the production plan, although frequently stated in different terms, should be in agreement with each other.

CAD/CAM The integration of Computer Aided Design and Computer Aided Manufacturing to achieve automation from design through manufacturing.

CAPACITY REQUIREMENTS PLANNING (CRP) The process of determining how much labor and/or machine resources are required to accomplish the tasks of production, and making plans to provide these resources. Open shop orders, as well as planned orders in the MRP system, are input to CRP which "translates" these orders into hours of work by work center by time period. In earlier years, the computer portion of CRP was called "infinite loading," a misnomer.

CLOSED LOOP MRP A system built around material requirements planning and also including the additional planning functions of production planning, master production scheduling, and capacity requirements planning. Further, once the planning phase is complete and the plans have been accepted as realistic and attainable, the execution functions come into play. These include the shop floor control functions of input/output measurement, dispatching, plus anticipated delay reports from both the shop and vendors, vendor scheduling, etc. The term "closed loop" implies that not only is each of these elements included in the overall system but also that there is feedback from the execution functions so that the planning can be kept valid at all times.

COMMON PARTS BILL (OF MATERIAL) A type of planning bill which groups all common components for a product or family of products into one bill of material.

CUMULATIVE LEAD TIME The longest length of time involved to accomplish the activity in question. For any item planned through MRP it is found by reviewing each bill of material path below the item, and whichever path adds up to the greatest number defines cumulative material lead time. Also called aggregate lead time, stacked lead time, composite lead time, critical path lead time.

CYCLE COUNTING A physical inventory-taking technique where

inventory is counted on a periodic schedule rather than once a year. For example, a cycle inventory count may be taken when an item reaches its reorder point, when new stock is received, or on a regular basis usually more frequently for high-value fast-moving items and less frequently for low-value or slow-moving items. Most effective cycle counting systems require the counting of a certain number of items every work day.

DAMPENERS   A technique within material requirements planning used to suppress the reporting of certain action messages created during the computer processing of MRP. Extensive use of dampeners is not recommended.

DEMAND   A need for a particular product or component. The demand could come from any number of sources, i.e., customer order, forecast, interplant, branch warehouse, service part, or to manufacture the next higher level. *See* Dependent demand, Independent demand.

DEMAND MANAGEMENT   The function of recognizing and managing all of the demands for products to ensure that the master scheduler is aware of them. It encompasses the activities of forecasting, order entry, order promising, branch warehouse requirements, interplant requirements, interplant orders, and service parts requirements.

DEMONSTRATED CAPACITY   Capacity calculated from actual performance data, usually number of items produced times standard hours per item plus the standard set-up time for each job.

DEPENDENT DEMAND   Demand is considered dependent when it comes from production schedules for other items. These demands should be calculated, not forecasted. A given item may have both dependent and independent demand at any given time. *See* Independent demand.

DIRECT-DEDUCT INVENTORY TRANSACTION PROCESSING   A method of doing bookkeeping which decreases the book (computer) inventory of an item as material is issued from stock, and increases the book inventory as material is received into stock. The key concept here is that the book record is updated coincident with the movement of material out of or into stock. As a result, the book record is a representation of what is physically in stock.

DISPATCH LIST   A listing of manufacturing orders in priority sequence according to the dispatching rules. The dispatch list is usually communicated to the manufacturing floor via hard copy or CRT display, and contains detailed information on priority, location, quantity, and the capacity requirements of the manufacturing order by operation. Dispatch lists are normally generated daily and oriented by work center. Also called the "daily foremen's report."

DISTRIBUTION CENTER   A warehouse with finished goods and/or service items. A typical company, for example, might have a manufacturing facility in Philadelphia and distribution centers in Atlanta, Dallas, Los Angeles, San Francisco, and Chicago. The term "distribution center" is synonymous with the term "branch warehouse," although the former has become more commonly used recently. When there is a warehouse that serves a group of satellite warehouses, this is usually called a regional distribution center.

DISTRIBUTION REQUIREMENTS PLANNING   The function of determining the needs to replenish inventory at branch warehouses. A time-phased order-point approach is used, where the planned orders at the branch warehouse level are "exploded" via MRP logic to become gross requirements on the supplying source. In the case of multilevel distribution networks, this explosion process can continue down through the various levels of master warehouse, factory warehouse, etc., and become input to the master production schedule. Demand on the supplying source(s) is recognized as dependent, and standard MRP logic applies.

DISTRIBUTION RESOURCE PLANNING (DRP)   The extension of Distribution Requirements Planning into the planning of the key resources contained in a distribution system: warehouse space, manpower, money, trucks and freight cars, etc.

FINAL ASSEMBLY SCHEDULE (FAS)   Also referred to as the "finishing schedule" as it may include other operations than simply the final operation. It is a schedule of end items either to replenish finished goods inventory or to finish the product for a make-to-order product. For make-to-order products, it is prepared after receipt of a customer order, is constrained by the availability of material and capacity, and it schedules the operations required to complete the product from the level where it is stocked (or master scheduled) to the end item level.

FINITE LOADING   Conceptually, the term means putting no more work into a work center than it can be expected to execute. The specific term usually refers to a computer technique that involves automatic shop priority revision in order to level load operation-by-operation. Successful applications of finite loading are very difficult to find.

FIRM PLANNED ORDER   A planned order that can be frozen in quantity and time. The computer is not allowed to change it; this is the responsibility of the planner in charge of the item. This technique can aid planners to respond to material and capacity problems by firming up selected planned orders. Firm planned orders are also the normal method of stating the master production schedule.

FIXED ORDER QUANTITY   An order quantity technique where the same quantity is planned to be ordered each time.

FLOW SHOP   A shop in which machines and operators handle a standard, usually uninterrupted material flow. The operators tend to perform the same operations for each production run. A flow shop is often referred to as a mass production shop, or is said to have a continuous manufacturing layout. The shop layout (arrangement of machines, benches, assembly lines, etc.) is designed to facilitate a product "flow." The process industries (chemicals, oil, paint, etc.) are extreme examples of flow shops. Each product, though variable in material specifications, uses the same flow pattern through the shop. See: job shop.

FOCUS FORECASTING   A system that allows the user to simulate the effectiveness of numerous forecasting techniques, thereby being able to select the most effective one.

FULL PEGGING   Refers to the ability of a system to automatically trace requirements for a given component all the way up to its ultimate end item (or contract number).

GENERALLY ACCEPTED MANUFACTURING PRACTICES A group of practices and principles, independent of any one set of techniques, which defines how a manufacturing company should be managed. Included are such elements as the need for data accuracy, frequent communications between marketing and manufacturing, top management control of the production planning process, systems capable of validly translating high-level plans into detailed schedules, etc.

GROUP TECHNOLOGY An engineering and manufacturing philosophy which identifies the "sameness" of parts, equipment or processes. It provides for rapid retrieval of existing designs and anticipates a cellular-type production equipment layout.

HEDGE 1) In master production scheduling, a quantity of stock used to protect against uncertainty in demand. The hedge is similar to safety stock, except that a hedge has the dimension of timing as well as amount. 2) In purchasing, any purchase or sale transaction having as its purpose the elimination of the negative aspects of price fluctuations.

INDEPENDENT DEMAND Demand for an item is considered independent when such demand is unrelated to the demand for other items. Demand for finished goods and service parts are examples of independent demand.

INFINITE LOADING *See* Capacity requirements planning.

INPUT/OUTPUT CONTROL A technique for capacity control where actual output from a work center is compared with the planned output (as developed by CRP and approved by Manufacturing). The input is also monitored to see if it corresponds with plans so that work centers will not be expected to generate output when jobs are not available to work on.

INTERPLANT DEMAND Material to be shipped to another plant or division within the corporation. Although it is not a customer order, it is usually handled by the master production scheduling system in a similar manner.

ITEM RECORD   The "master" record for an item. Typically it contains identifying and descriptive data, control values (lead times, lot order quantities, etc.) and may contain data on inventory status, requirements, and planned orders. Item records are linked together by bill of material records (or product structure records), thus defining the bill of material.

JOB SHOP   A functional organization whose departments or work centers are organized around particular types of equipment or operations, such as drilling, forging, spinning, or assembly. Products move through departments by individual shop orders.

JUST-IN-TIME   In the narrow sense, a method of execution designed to result in minimum inventory by having material arrive at each operation just in time to be used. In the broad sense, it refers to all the activities of manufacturing which make the just-in-time movement of material possible, with the ultimate goal being elimination of waste. Just-in-time is possible via MRP II or, in some cases, via Kanban.

KANBAN   A scheduling approach which uses standard containers with a card attached to each. Developed in Japan, it has been used in certain highly repetitive manufacturing environments to achieve Just-In-Time. Loosely translated, Kanban means "card," or more literally, "billboard" or "sign."

LEAD TIME   A span of time required to perform an activity. In a logistics context, the activity in question is normally the procurement of materials and/or products either from an outside supplier or from one's own manufacturing facility. The individual components of any given lead time can include some or all of the following: order preparation time, queue time, move or transportation time, receiving and inspection time.

LEVEL   Every part of assembly in a product structure is assigned a level code signifying the relative level in which that part or assembly is used within that product structure. Normally, the end items are assigned level "0" and the components/subassemblies going into it are level "1" and so on. The MRP explosion process starts from level "0" and proceeds downwards one level at a time.

LOAD   The amount of scheduled work ahead of a manufacturing facility, usually expressed in terms of hours of work or units of production.

LOGISTICS   In an industrial context, this term refers to the functions of obtaining and distributing material and product. In a military sense (where it has greater usage), its meaning can also include the transportation of personnel.

LOT-FOR-LOT   An order quantity technique in MRP which generates planned orders in quantities equal to the net requirements in each period. Also called discrete, one-for-one.

MACHINE LOADING   The accumulation by work centers of the hours generated from the scheduling of operations for released orders by time period. Machine loading differs from capacity requirements planning in that it does not use the planned orders from MRP but operates solely for scheduled receipts. As such, it has very limited usefulness.

MAKE-TO-ORDER PRODUCT   The end item is finished after receipt of a customer order. Frequently, long lead-time components are planned prior to the order arriving in order to reduce the delivery time to the customer. Where options or other subassemblies are stocked prior to customer orders arriving, the term "assemble-to-order" is frequently used.

MAKE-TO-STOCK PRODUCT   The end item is shipped from finished goods "off the shelf," and therefore, is finished prior to a customer order arriving.

MANUFACTURING RESOURCE PLANNING (MRP II)   A method for the effective planning of all resources of a manufacturing company. Ideally, it addresses operational planning in units, financial planning in dollars, and has a simulation capability to answer "what if" questions. It is made up of a variety of functions, each linked together: business planning, production planning, master production scheduling, material requirements planning, capacity requirements planning and the execution support systems for capacity and material. Output from these systems would be integrated with financial reports such as the business plan, purchase commitment reports, shipping budget, inventory projections in dollars, etc. Manufacturing Resource Planning is a direct outgrowth and extension of closed loop MRP. MRP II has also been defined, validly, as a management system based on network scheduling. Also, and perhaps best, as organized common sense.

MASTER PRODUCTION SCHEDULE (MPS) The anticipated build schedule. The master scheduler maintains this schedule and, in turn, it becomes a set of planning numbers which "drives" MRP. It represents what the company plans to produce expressed in specific configurations, quantities and dates. The master production schedule must take into account customer orders and forecasts, backlog, availability of material, availability of capacity, management policy and goals, etc.

MATERIAL REQUIREMENTS PLANNING (MRP) A set of techniques which uses bills of material, inventory data and the master production schedule to calculate requirements for materials. It makes recommendations to release replenishment orders for material. Further, since it is time phased, it makes recommendations to reschedule open orders when due dates and need dates are not in phase. Originally seen as merely a better way to order inventory, today it is thought of primarily as a scheduling technique, i.e., a method for establishing and maintaining valid due dates on orders. It is the foundation for closed loop MRP.

MATERIALS MANAGEMENT An organizational structure which groups the functions related to the complete cycle of material flow, from the purchase and internal control of production materials to the planning and control of work-in-process to the warehousing, shipping and distribution of the finished product.

MODULAR BILL (OF MATERIAL) A type of planning bill which is arranged in product modules or options. Often used in companies where the product has many optional features, e.g., automobiles. *See* Planning bill.

MURPHY'S LAW A tongue-in-cheek observation which states: "If anything can go wrong, it will."

NET CHANGE MRP A method of processing material requirements planning on the computer whereby the material plan is continually retained in the computer. Whenever there is a change in requirements, open order or inventory status, bills of material, etc., a partial explosion is made only for those parts affected by the change.

NET REQUIREMENTS In MRP, the net requirements for a part or an assembly are derived as a result of netting gross requirements against inventory on hand and the scheduled receipts. Net requirements, lot sized and offset for lead time, become planned orders.

ON-HAND BALANCE The quantity shown in the inventory records as being physically in stock.

OPEN ORDER An active manufacturing order or purchase order. *See* Scheduled receipts.

OPTION A choice or feature offered to customers for customizing the end product. In many companies, the term "option" means a mandatory choice, i.e., the customer must select from one of the available choices. For example, in ordering a new car, the customer must specify an engine (option) but need not necessarily select an air conditioner.

ORDER ENTRY The process of accepting and translating what a customer wants into terms used by the manufacturer. This can be as simple as creating shipping documents for a finished goods product to a far more complicated series of activities including engineering effort for make-to-order products.

ORDER PROMISING The process of making a delivery commitment, i.e., answering the question "When can you ship?" For make-to-order products, this usually involves a check of material and capacity availability.

ORDER QUANTITY The amount of an item to be ordered. Also called lot size.

PEGGING In MRP, pegging displays, for a given item, the details of the sources of its gross requirements and/or allocations. Pegging can be thought of as "live" where-used information.

PERIOD ORDER QUANTITY An order quantity technique under which the order quantity will be equal to the net requirements for a given number of periods (e.g., weeks) into the future. Also called days' supply, weeks' supply, fixed period.

PICKING   The process of issuing components to the production floor on a job-by-job basis. Also called kitting.

PICKING LIST   A document which is used to pick manufacturing orders, listing the components and quantities required.

PLANNED ORDER   A suggested order quantity and due date created by MRP processing, when it encounters net requirements. Planned orders are created by the computer, exist only within the computer, and may be changed or deleted by the computer during subsequent MRP processing if conditions change. Planned orders at one level will be exploded into gross requirements for components at the next lower level. Planned orders also serve as input to capacity requirements planning, along with scheduled receipts, to show the total capacity requirements in future time periods.

PLANNER/BUYER   *See* Vendor scheduler.

PLANNING BILL (OF MATERIAL)   An artificial grouping of items and/or events, in bill of material format, used to facilitate master scheduling and/or material planning. A modular bill of material is one type of planning bill.

POST-DEDUCT INVENTORY TRANSACTION PROCESSING   A method of doing inventory bookkeeping where the book (computer) inventory of components is reduced only after completion of activity on their upper level parent or assembly. This approach has the disadvantage of a built-in differential between the book record and what is physically in stock. Also called backflush.

PRE-DEDUCT INVENTORY TRANSACTION PROCESSING   A method of doing inventory bookkeeping where the book (computer) inventory of components is reduced prior to issue, at the time of scheduled receipt for their parent or assembly is created. This approach has the disadvantage of a built-in differential between the book record and what is physically in stock.

PRODUCT STRUCTURE   *See* Bill of material.

PRODUCTION PLANNING   The function of setting the overall level of manufacturing output. Its prime purpose is to establish production rates that will achieve management's objective in terms of raising or lowering inventories or backlogs, while usually attempting to keep the production force relatively stable. The production plan is usually stated in broad terms (e.g., product groupings, families of products). It must extend through a planning horizon sufficient to plan the labor, equipment, facilities, material and finances required to accomplish the production plan. Various units of measure are used by different companies to express the plan such as standard hours, tonnage, labor operators, units, pieces, etc. As this plan affects all company functions, it is normally prepared with information from marketing, manufacturing, engineering, finance, materials, etc. In turn, the production plan becomes management's authorization for the master scheduler to convert into a more detailed plan.

PROJECTED AVAILABLE BALANCE   The inventory balance projected out into the future. It is the running sum of on-hand inventory, minus requirements, plus scheduled receipts and (usually) planned orders.

QUEUE   A waiting line. In manufacturing the jobs at a given work center waiting to be processed. As queues increase, so do average lead times and work-in-process inventories.

QUEUE TIME   The amount of time a job waits at a work center before set-up or work is performed on the job. Queue time is one element of total manufacturing lead time. Increases in queue time result in direct increases to manufacturing lead time.

REGENERATION MRP   A method of processing material requirements planning on the computer whereby the master production schedule is totally re-exploded down through all bills of material, at least once per week to maintain valid priorities. New requirements and planned orders are completely "regenerated" at that time.

REPETITIVE MANUFACTURING   Production of discrete units, planned and executed via schedule, usually at relatively high speeds and volumes. Material tends to move in a sequential flow. *See* Flow shop.

RESCHEDULING ASSUMPTION   A fundamental piece of MRP logic which assumes that existing open orders can be rescheduled in nearer time periods far more easily than new orders can be released and received. As a result, planned order receipts are not created until all scheduled receipts have been applied to cover gross requirements.

RESOURCE REQUIREMENTS PLANNING *See* Rough-cut capacity planning.

ROUGH-CUT CAPACITY PLANNING The process of converting the production plan and/or the master production schedule into capacity needs for key resources: manpower, machinery, warehouse space, vendors' capabilities and in some cases, money. Product load profiles are often used to accomplish this. The purpose of rough-cut capacity planning is to evaluate the plan prior to attempting to implement it. Sometimes called resource requirements planning.

ROUTING A document detailing the manufacture of a particular item. It includes the operations to be performed, their sequence, the various work centers to be involved, and the standards for set-up and run. In some companies, the routing also includes information on tooling, operator skill levels, inspection operations, testing requirements, etc.

SAFETY STOCK In general, a quantity of stock planned to be available to protect against fluctuations in demand and/or supply.

SAFETY TIME A technique in MRP whereby material is planned to arrive ahead of the requirement date. The difference between the requirement date and the planned in-stock-date is safety time.

SCHEDULED RECEIPTS Within MRP, open production orders and open purchase orders are considered as "scheduled receipts" on their due date and will be treated as part of available inventory during the netting process for the time period in question. Scheduled receipt dates and/or quantities are not normally altered automatically by the computer. Further, scheduled receipts are not exploded into requirements for components, as MRP logic assumes that all components required for the manufacture of the item in question have either been allocated or issued to the shop floor.

SCRAP FACTOR A percentage factor used by MRP to increase gross requirements of a given component to account for anticipated loss of that component during the manufacture of its parent.

SERVICE PARTS Parts used for the repair and/or maintenance of a product. Also called repair parts, spares.

SHOP FLOOR CONTROL A system for utilizing data from the shop floor as well as data processing files to maintain and communicate status information on shop orders (manufacturing orders) and work centers. The major subfunctions of shop floor control are: 1) assigning priority of each shop order, 2) maintaining work-in-process quantity information, 3) conveying shop order status information, 4) providing actual input and output data for capacity control purposes, 5) providing quantity by location by shop order for work-in-process inventory and accounting purposes, 6) providing measurement of efficiency, utilization and productivity of manpower and machines.

SHOP ORDER CLOSE-OUT STATION A stocking point on the shop floor. Completed production of components is transacted (received) into the shop order close-out station and subsequently transacted (issued) to assembly or other "downstream" operations. This technique is used to reduce material handling by not having to move items into and out of stockrooms, while simultaneously enabling a high degree of inventory record accuracy.

SHRINKAGE FACTOR A factor used in material requirements planning which compensates for expected loss during the manufacturing cycle either by increasing the gross requirements or by reducing the expected completion quantity of planned and open orders. The shrinkage factor differs from the scrap factor in that the former affects all uses of the part and its components. The scrap relates to only one usage.

SIMULATION Within MRP II, utilizing the operational date to perform "what-if" evaluations of alternative plans, to answer the question "Can we do it?" If yes, the simulation can then be run in financial mode to help answer the question "Do we really want to?"

TIME BUCKET A number of days of data summarized into one columnar display. A weekly time bucket in MRP would contain all the relevant planning data for an entire week. Weekly time buckets are considered to be the largest possible (at least in the near- and medium-term) to permit effective MRP.

TIME FENCE   Point in time where various restrictions or changes in operating procedures take place. For example, changes to the master production schedule can be accomplished easily beyond the cumulative lead time; whereas, changes inside the cumulative lead time become increasingly more difficult, to a point where changes should be resisted. Time fences can be used to define these points.

TWO-LEVEL MPS   A master scheduling approach for make-to-order products where an end product type is master scheduled along with selected key options, features, attachments and common parts.

TURNOVER   The number of times inventory is replaced during a time period; in other words, a measurement of investment inventory to support a given level of sales. It is found by dividing the cost of goods sold for the period by the average inventory for the period.

VENDOR SCHEDULER   A person whose main job is working with vendors regarding what's needed and when. Vendor schedulers are in direct contact with both MRP and the vendors. They do the material planning for the items under their control, communicate the resultant schedules to their assigned vendors, do follow-up, resolve problems, etc. The vendor schedulers are normally organized by commodity, as are the buyers. By using the vendor scheduler approach, the buyers are freed from day-to-day order placement and expediting, and therefore have the time to do cost reduction, negotiation, vendor selection, alternate sourcing, etc. Another term for vendor scheduler is planner/buyer.

VENDOR SCHEDULING   A purchasing approach which provides vendors with schedules rather than individual hard-copy purchase orders. Normally a vendor scheduling system will include a business agreement (contract) for each vendor, a weekly schedule for each vendor extending for some time into the future, and individuals called vendor schedulers. Also required is a formal priority planning system that works very well, because it is essential in this arrangement to provide the vendor with valid due dates routinely.

WORK-IN-PROCESS   Product in various stages of completion

throughout the plant, including raw material that has been released for initial processing and completely processed material awaiting final inspection and acceptance as finished product or shipment to a customer. Many accounting systems also include semi-finished stock and components in this category.

ZERO INVENTORIES A term adopted by APICS (American Production & Inventory Control Society), the meaning of which is similar to Just-In-Time.

Index